JAMES QUINNETT
Memories Time Can't Heal
A Vietnam War Novel

First published by Guthrie-Pierce Publishing 2024

Copyright © 2024 by James Quinnett

All rights reserved. No part of this publication may be reproduced, stored or transmitted in any form or by any means, electronic, mechanical, photocopying, recording, scanning, or otherwise without written permission from the publisher. It is illegal to copy this book, post it to a website, or distribute it by any other means without permission.

James Quinnett asserts the moral right to be identified as the author of this work.

The novel is set in the central highlands and I Corp of Vietnam, among other actual places. Novels need villains and heroes, which are invented in this novel. I served under four fine company commanders, two of whom were killed in action, and with men who were remarkably skilled and brave infantrymen. The situations, incidents, and dialogues concerning those persons are entirely fictional and are not intended to depict actual events or persons or to change the entirely fictional nature of the work. In all other respects, any resemblance to an actual person, living or dead, events, or locales is entirely coincidental.

First edition

ISBN: 979-8-9899292-0-7

Editing by Laura Dragonette
Proofreading by Ray Braun
Cover art by David Ter-Avanesyan

This book was professionally typeset on Reedsy. Find out more at reedsy.com

For Nancy

Contents

I Part One

1 The Hilton Inn   3

II Part Two

2 A Year Ago   9
3 An Khê   15
4 Ambushed   19
5 The Bridge   27
6 Situation Report   30
7 Awards Day   35
8 Lanny Jr.   37
9 Captain Carter   40
10 Moving Out   43
11 Her Charge   49
12 LZ English   51
13 Binh Dinh Province   54
14 Dak To   57
15 Kontum   70
16 Policing the Locals   76
17 Screaming Eagles   79
18 Candyland   84

19	Bored	87
20	Mad Minute	90
21	Taipei	94
22	Welcome to the I Corps	103
23	Eight-ball	108
24	Ambushed Again	112
25	Dane	116
26	The Foot	120
27	Letter from Home	123
28	Casey's Peeing Adventure	126
29	The Spider Hole	129
30	The Card Game	133
31	Hot LZ	136
32	The Graveyard	142
33	Up in Flames	146
34	Body Bags	152
35	Leaving for An Khê	164
36	Japan	171
37	Cam Ranh Bay	184
III	Part Three	
38	Uncle Nick	191
39	Helen	195
40	Mrs. Smith	197
41	The Letter	202

I

Part One

1

The Hilton Inn

Seated in the back seat of the army transport van, I peered out of the back window at the car headlights following us. They were searching the highway for what I had no clue. As they passed, red taillights seemed to signal caution. It was twilight, and I was sandwiched between two worlds. The weather felt cold and damp against my skin for a change. Two hours ago, I had ingested a steak dinner, a welcome-home offering provided courtesy of the United States Army.

I was dressed in army greens, thanks to a newly minted uniform issued at Fort Lewis, Washington—earned ribbons, name tag, crossed rifles pin on the lapel, shiny black shoes. I'd stepped into a world that had lived only in my mind for the last twelve months. The pace, the fast-moving cars, everything out of step—everything was moving so fast. I wondered where they were going. Did they even know where they were going? Why were they going so fast? What was all that important? It just felt weird and foreign.

The flight from the Seattle-Tacoma airport to San Francisco was short compared to the long trip from Cam Ranh Bay. After checking into the Hilton and hauling my duffel bag up to the room, I decided to get a drink.

My eyes took in the rich and excessive atmosphere of the hotel restaurant—wrong somehow. A band was playing at the far end. A few other chaps like me floated about in similar garb, but most were in civilian clothes, living the good life. Out of danger and without a care in the world, fellow travelers were wrapped in a blanket of security, sipping highballs, the men playing pocket pool and laughing. I hated them. I should have gone AWOL in Japan when we stopped there to refuel.

As I found a stool and sat down at the bar, I stared at the image of myself in the mirror. I ordered a draft and my mind started to wander—the thought of the past year, the carnage. The image of a boy serving me my last beer in the Nam, his face melted by napalm, flashed through my mind. I studied my image in the mirror; the Air Medal on my chest caught my eye. I was proud of that one. You had to fly twenty-five missions for that one. Then the Combat Infantry Badge; you had to have been in combat for at least thirty days for that one. I was proud, conflicted, and confused; the beer in front of me seemed wholly inadequate.

As I looked around, I realized no one here really gave a shit. They were dressed in comfortable clothes, sipping their drinks, eating their steaks, and making their money with their only worry being investments.

"Can I sit here?" a voice asked.

I looked up and noticed a kindred spirit with sandy blond hair, a stocky fellow with a round face and innocent eyes, a fellow soldier, also slightly out of place in this opulent environment.

"Sure, have a seat," I said.

He pulled out the stool and sat down. "Where you from?" I asked.

"Kansas, western Kansas. How about you?" he asked.

"Southern Cal, San Bernardino," I answered. "What do you do there in western Kansas?"

THE HILTON INN

"Mainly farming, wheat and cattle."

From his single ribbon—Good Conduct—I surmised he was bait for the cause.

"What's your name?" I asked.

"Jerome, Jerome Richardson," he said.

"Where you headed?" I asked as if I didn't know.

"Vietnam," he answered.

"Yeah, well, I just got back from there today," I said.

"Wow, what's it like?" he said.

"It's no walk in the park, I can tell you." I could see from the crossed rifles on his lapel he was infantry. Judging from his size, I figured a machine gun was probably in his future.

"Where'd you train?" I asked.

"Tigerland."

"Me too."

Suffering from jet lag and sleep deprivation, I thought of Japan and the restaurant on the top floor of the hotel where I was staying. Scott McKenzie's song "San Francisco" flashed through my mind. "Gentle people with flowers in their hair." And here I was, in San Francisco, having a drink with my replacement. Poor bastard.

"Scared?"

"Yeah," he said, then fell silent.

"It'll be all right," I said, knowing 500 guys a week were being sent home in body bags. With the Tet Offensive in full swing, the whole fucking country was in flames. Yeah, it'll be all right, my ass.

The band started playing "(Sittin' on) the Dock of the Bay." *Wow, never heard that before. Shit, that's good stuff. What else have I missed?* Fucking weird, having taken a snapshot out of the window of a commercial jet with my Kodak Instamatic of two C-130s at the ready on the tarmac in Cam Ranh Bay on February 10, and—because of the international date line—being discharged from active duty and sucking up suds at

5

the Hilton the same day. I woke up in the Nam and would be going to bed back in the world.

I glanced down at the ringworm on my hand—a parting gift, you might say—and I wondered if Jerome would make it. Would he come home in one piece or zipped up in a body bag? Would he be just another baby killer in the making? Maybe he'd earn the title and wear it proudly. And would he be able to survive the guilt if he did make it? Perhaps he'd be a stoner, a drunk, a rapist. How soon would the shackles of civilization peel away? Would his moral compass go south on day one or day three hundred? All I knew was he might get out of the Nam standing up, but he wouldn't get away free. Like a cattle brand, images of horror, the smell of burning flesh and shit, and the cries of innocents would burn into his brain. It might scab over, but it wouldn't heal.

We shared the expense of the room I already had and parted ways after breakfast.

"Good luck," I said and slipped my name and address, written on the hotel notepad, into his hand. "Let me know where you end up."

We shook hands. Looking into his eyes, I knew they'd see things only I and others like me would understand a year from now. Jerome left in search of transportation to Alameda and processing, and I went to find the PSA ticket counter to purchase airfare to LA.

II

Part Two

2

A Year Ago

I grabbed the handrail of the stairs leading to the open door of the aircraft, my foot no longer resting on US soil. Two hostesses at the top of the landing greeted us dressed in snappy tan outfits, skirts reaching just below the knee, with mushroom-style bonnets resting on their heads—like a cherry plopped on top of a banana split. World Airways had contracted to ferry us the next seventeen hours to Vietnam, the end of the line, a one-way ticket courtesy of Uncle Sam.

Twenty minutes into the flight, I looked out the window—now a few thousand feet in the air—the land trading places with the ocean. We were chasing the sun.

Finally, the OK to smoke sign lit up on the console. From inside my breast pocket, I pulled out a pack of Marlboros, fished a filtered cigarette out, and lit up, taking a deep drag.

Dewey Watkins, sitting next to me, turned and exclaimed, "I'm from Chattanooga!" Then he added, "Tennessee. Where are you from?"

Taking another drag, I answered him in an absent-minded fashion. "Rialto, Southern California." Lost in my thoughts of home and the unknown, I always answered that question the same way, distinguishing between the northern and the southern parts of the state.

"Wow, what's it like there? Is Rialto on the beach?" Dewey peppered me with questions.

Not really up for a conversation, I answered, "Oh, it's OK. And, no, it's not on the beach, and I've never met Frankie Avalon or Annette Funicello." His questions started to irritate me, and I just didn't feel like dealing with him.

His mood soured. And he left me alone.

As the hours went by and the conversations started up again, I found Dewey—sandy-colored hair, peach fuzz for whiskers, front teeth that didn't grow in straight—a likable sort. I got to where I enjoyed his descriptions of Chattanooga and the Tennessee River that nearly circles it, the ships, and the so-called views from Rock City. According to him, you can see forever. Adding a bonus feature, he said, "You can grow practically anything in that Tennessee soil."

I had the window seat; Dewey was sandwiched in the middle between me and the little prick, Skip. I already didn't like the bastard nervously fidgeting in his aisle seat. After hours holed up in a jet, you kinda get to know the guys next to you, whether you like it or not. Skip, with a crooked nose and beady blue eyes, was running his mouth nonstop. He annoyed the crap out of me, talking trash from the get-go. Dewey took the brunt of it—bad luck. If Skip wasn't talking about killing, he was talking about Alabama football and Bear Bryant.

In the middle of the night, after a brief stop at Clark Air Base for refueling—the third leg of the journey—we took off for a short two hours to the Nam. For some, I'm sure it was their last destination in an upright position.

The ground crew positioned the stairs at the front door of the Boeing 707 at the Tan Son Nhut airport. Dewey, Skip, and I and our fellow travelers, dressed in khaki short-sleeve shirts and long pants with cunt caps perched atop our heads, made our way down the stairs. On Asian soil for the first time, we were FNGs—fucking new guys.

A YEAR AGO

It was still nighttime, the sun having escaped hours ago, and the realization that I'd arrived in a war zone was overwhelming. The intermittent illumination rounds fired into the black skies, exploding; parachutes opening high above the ground, floating down like leaves on a late autumn day. Only these leaves had flares hanging from them, swinging back and forth in the breeze, causing our shadows to dance on the tarmac. We headed for the buses. Finding a seat, I noticed the windows had heavy gauge wire covering them. I pondered the reasons why and peered through the wire, surveilling the houses and streets as we made our way to Long Binh, the 90th Replacement Battalion. With the unfamiliar smells wafting through the air, I sat transfixed by the silent, sleepy streets and the occasional naked light bulb hanging in the structures we passed by. Nothing felt real. It was all foreign, new, and forbidding.

As we settled into our new digs, Skip started in again.

He turned to Dewey. "Yeah, I'm going to put a major hurt on them motherfuckers. I can't wait to get my hands on a rifle. You just wait, this badass is going to fuck 'em up good."

Jesus Christ! Is that little prick ever going to shut up? I figured he was lucky when he found a low-hanging urinal so he wouldn't have to use the stall.

I once worked with a guy like that named Henry Tuttle, in the tin mill lab back at Kaiser Steel. The same line of bullshit, his chest puffed up like a bullfrog looking for a mate. He supposedly shot down five MiGs during the Korean War. In great detail, he'd described the dog fights and just barely making it back to base after each encounter. We all figured he was full of it, but when it occurred to us metallurgical lab rats that he would have been eleven years old, the lie was exposed. Henry never said much after that.

Day one in the Nam and all we did was write Mom, Pop, and girlfriends at the request of the army. Put family and friends' minds at ease. Let them know you've arrived safe and sound in a shit storm.

I was feeling a little bummed out and turned to Dewey and remarked, "I hate being in limbo, wish we knew where we are going. It'd be good to know what outfit some pencil dick was going to assign us."

"Ain't nobody knows," Dewey responded.

Late in the afternoon, a sergeant entered the barracks and said, "We need a few volunteers for guard duty." Silence filled the barracks momentarily. Sitting on the edge of my bunk, I said nothing, along with most everyone else. Lesson one, never volunteer. But, of course, a few bozos did.

Skip, being the gung ho bastard, answered in the affirmative, "Yo, sign me up, Sergeant!"

Skip left the barracks for his shift around twenty-two hundred hours. The other volunteers left sometime during the night, according to their assigned times.

On day two, Larry, a big kid with room-temperature IQ (not too bad considering we were in the tropics), while sitting in the chow hall eating breakfast—coffee, eggs, and a bit of what might pass as sausage—asked the table full of green-clad FNGs: "Did you hear about the dumb-ass shooting himself in the leg last night?"

Everyone was pausing with forks and spoons in hand, waiting on the details. "No," I said.

"Nearly blew his goddamn leg off."

As Larry fumbled for words, choking down another bite of sausage, he continued, "I don't think he meant to, but who knows. You got to be fucked up in the head to put a bullet in your leg."

"I bet he didn't figure on that." I mused. *Geez, how scared do you have to be to shoot yourself? How fucked up would you have to be to pull the trigger?*

"Who was it, do you know?" I asked.

"I think his name was Skip, Skippy . . . something like that."

It was afternoon; the barracks emptied into the courtyard for assignments. Dress right, dress, stand at ease, wait for your name to be called.

"When I call your name, sound off, and take one step forward," barked the sergeant.

"Yes, Sergeant!" we yelled in unison.

"The following soldiers are assigned to the Big Red One."

He didn't speak my name that day or the next when they announced assignments to the 25th Infantry. I was hoping for the 25th. It seemed to me from what little information we could pick up back in Tigerland that the 25th was the best of a no-win situation.

After being dismissed, while casually walking back to the barracks—the chow line wouldn't start forming for another hour—I asked Dewey, "Did you ever run into a sergeant by the name of Nelson, a fat guy with a limp back in Tigerland? He had that big First Cav patch on his sleeve."

"No, not really."

"He was weird, not very talkative, stayed to himself—looked fucked up somehow. Sure wouldn't want to be assigned to that outfit."

On the third day, we were once again ordered out to the courtyard. This time, the sergeant major, standing on the same three-foot-high wooden platform as yesterday and the day before, under the still-burning sun, called the names destined for the 1st Air Cavalry Division.

One of the last names to be called, I sounded off and took a step forward, thinking I was fucked. A future Sergeant Nelson, wounds and squirrelly behavior, that was my fucking future. Great! Dewey was right there with me.

It was late afternoon and all of us draftees scooped up off the streets of the US—answering the call—grabbed our duffel bags and headed to the small plane. They called it a Caribou, with a ramp allowing you to enter the rear of the aircraft. I crawled up the plane's butt thinking there was a first time for everything. Unlike a commercial jet with all the seats facing the future, all pointed in the direction we were flying, in these seats, we faced each other. Rather than glimpsing a look at the blue sky outside or the back of someone's head, we faced the fear in each other's eyes. I was the last one in. Pulling down the seat, adjusting my duffel bag between my legs, I looked toward the flight cabin, everyone busy assuming the same position. The engines started roaring, the blades twisting through the evening air, as I stared directly across from me now: red vinyl straps crisscrossed vertically and horizontally a few inches from the wall of the fuselage, and an empty seat still folded up.

3

An Khê

A crusty old sergeant greeted us under the midmorning sun. As newly assigned FNGs, we fell into formation in front of the company's orderly room. The sergeant read from the manifest with a sour attitude, calling our names and designating our platoons. As we made our way to our respective barracks, the smell of BO from the old-timers filled the air; they had just returned after spending a couple of months in the field.

Carrying my duffel bag, I found my temporary home and looked down the length of the structure, which was made of pine with slats for ventilation and naked light bulbs, a barracks filled with crazy motherfuckers. The guys appeared almost like shadowy figures dancing—twitchy bastards. They were in a jubilant mood, messing with shit in their footlockers—personal stuff they hadn't seen in a while—and telling stories about the village in flames. The barracks were lined with bunk beds on both sides with footlockers: one at the foot of the bunk, the other against the wall. One guy pulled up his shirt to show Dewey his scars from an earlier firefight, knowing full well it would fuck with his head. Others were laughing and bragging about how fast the thatched roofs burned. These fuckers were scary, and they were enjoying the moment. It didn't seem like there was anything civilized about them—they were more like wild animals bearing invisible teeth and protecting their turf. Was this my future?

How do you get to know a bunch of crazies? To know the hell they've gone through. I knew a baptism of sorts was required to join the soulless fraternity.

The next couple of nights were filled with going to the club and drinking beer. Barry, a Yankee from upstate New York, heard a rumor that some of our comrades had killed a couple of guys from the artillery unit in the barracks across the road from us. Evidently, it was some sort of drunken disagreement about nothing in particular that caused the incident. I didn't know if it was true, but it just further illustrated the bizarre nature of things, space, and time that didn't compute.

Morning broke, and the cocksucking sergeant yelled for us to get up like the morning before and the morning before that. That's the one thing you can count on in the rear, some asshole busting your chops for sleeping. Of course, that was nothing new. On this morning, all us newbies reported in front of the orderly room for training—some place close to where they take you out for a test run in the bush. The trucks—deuce and a halves—were running late.

Just north of base camp, after a couple of klicks, the trucks deposited us in an open field. After we spent three days setting up camp, eating C rations, and stumbling around in relative safety, the army figured we were ready for go time. By the time we finished training and got back to the company area, the old-timers were gone.

AN KHÊ

It was our last night of drinking, and all the speculation would disappear in the next twenty-four hours. It was our last night before boarding a Chinook headed for LZ English and the unknown.

Freddie and I grabbed a table after ordering a couple of beers from the bar. We were a year or two older than the other draftees. With the dim light and the pine slats allowing a breeze to flow through, I asked my drinking buddy, "Where are you from back in the world?"

"Iowa," Freddie said.

"Whereabouts in Iowa?" I asked.

"Fort Dodge."

What were the odds I'd meet up with a kid from Fort Dodge?

"I know Fort Dodge. I remember going to a rodeo there once when I was a kid. My grandfather had a farm about twenty miles south of there. It was just north of a little town called Stratford. Every other summer, we'd go visit him."

"Yeah, that is a coincidence," Freddie said. "Does he still live there?"

"No, unfortunately. A couple of years back, he was visiting us in California when he started having chest pains. The folks called the doctor to come by the house and check on him. After a brief examination, he called my folks into a back room to discuss his condition. I was watching him lying on the couch when he strained as if trying to take a breath. It was his last. I was a senior in high school at the time."

"That sucks," Freddie said.

"Yeah, it did," I said.

After a lull in the conversation and realizing that the hours of relative safety were slipping away, we headed back to the barracks to catch some shut-eye. I thought about the discussion we'd had about the merits of fighting this war. Both of us had moved around, attending various colleges to postpone the draft. We were trying to gum up the paperwork for our respective draft boards. But, in the end, Uncle Sam nabbed us both. Freddie believed in the war, and I did not. We agreed on one thing: neither one of us wanted to fight it.

4

Ambushed

Upon landing and exiting from the rear of the Chinook, I must have looked lost when Sergeant Morgan asked, "Looking for Alpha Company?"

He must have been clairvoyant. "Yes, Sergeant," I answered.

With a quick smile, the sergeant said, "Follow me."

The other members of the communications unit were sitting in a circle discarding unwanted cards and drawing new ones from a poncho liner draped over a stack of C rations. I figured the game for poker.

After being assigned to the communications unit and not knowing shit about being a radio operator, I was hoping to pick up the lingo and details of the job in short order. Lieutenant Turner, the executive officer, agreed to take me on as his RTO.

Sergeant Morgan had a calm smile, with a happy-go-lucky personality. Ryan Birdsong, Robert Rayshell, Gary Hatfield, and Casey—I didn't catch his last name—introduced themselves and then turned their attention back to the game.

"You hear about the two guys that drowned in the rice paddy?" Ryan asked me, looking for a facial response. Then he fanned his cards and said, "Poor bastards."

"Beat that, you motherfuckers," shouted Casey, laying down a straight, Jack high.

I said nothing for a second, then added in response to Ryan, "No, I hadn't heard." Evidently, they'd drowned when a personnel carrier slipped off the road and pinned them in a rice paddy.

Hatfield, picking up his cards, said, "That's fucked up." After winning the next hand, he shuffled the deck.

Ryan continued, "You're a lucky man. We got some easy duty here. No fucking around with those fucking gook villages or humping the countryside."

I relaxed a little and watched the poker game and listened to the banter.

An hour, maybe two, and Morgan began assigning radio watch for the night. The game ended, and Hatfield called in the SIT-REP (situation report: personnel strength, supplies needed, etc.) to battalion headquarters.

I had just gotten my air mattress blown up and squared away when a call came from battalion headquarters asking to talk to the captain. Hatfield answered and hauled his radio over to the captain's hooch.

Hatfield came back a few minutes later and announced, "Pack up your shit, we're moving out."

I could hear the Chinooks approaching from LZ English moments later. It was dark now, and everyone was scrambling to get their shit together. I didn't have all that much stuff since the supply sergeant back at English was out of rucksacks, so he issued me a fanny pack, poncho, air mattress, ammo, and canteens. That's all I had to pack.

There were no explanations of where we were going or why. I could tell everyone was a little nervous and on edge. It's not every day you move out on such short notice, especially at night, according to Hatfield. At this point, I thought maybe they were all full of shit when it came to forecasting the future. Word spread that Bravo Company was mixing it up with the Cong at the north end of An Lao Valley, and we were being called in for support.

At LZ English, we transferred from Chinooks to Hueys. As we lifted into the air again, it was dark and moonless, the only light coming from the occasional burning structures below. It was eerie and surreal, and I hoped the Huey would just keep going. But no, we started descending until we were hovering over a rice paddy. I was riding shotgun and slid the door back, catching the door gunner off guard. I must have smashed his hand between the door and his machine gun. He yelled, "God damn it, motherfucker," as I jumped into the rice paddy, sinking into the mud up to my knees. I was hoping the suction from the mud wouldn't pull my boots off as I tried to follow the others. It crossed my mind that if it were a hot LZ, we'd be fucked. Chopper after chopper hovered just long enough until the entire company was slogging through the mud toward solid ground. We found our way to a large grassy area surrounded by thatched-roof houses. Dispensing with the routine of blowing up air mattresses and snapping together ponchos, we slept on the grass as best we could. I could hear sporadic gunfire a couple of klicks to the north, but eventually, I closed my eyes and slept.

With the morning light—what photographers call the golden hour—the greens were greener, the blue sky bluer, plus the temperature was comfortable. I'd not been in the field twenty-four hours, and already I'd flown my first combat mission.

Captain Kahele, looking like a happy Buddha with a flattop, was propped up against the trunk of a tree. He'd sent word that he wanted to see me. I think he was Hawaiian, maybe a Pacific Islander. The morning light made his round bronze face shine.

In an obviously caring manner, the captain asked, "How are you doing, Private?"

"Fine, sir," I said.

"I just wanted to welcome you to Alpha Company and let you know you'll do just fine."

"Thank you, sir."

As I turned and crossed the lush green grass dotted with trees and stucco houses with thatched roofs spaced appropriately—idyllic somehow—I thought it strange that the captain would take an interest in a newbie like me. But I welcomed the interest—he seemed like a nice guy, and I appreciated his effort. Just maybe, he was right, and everything would be all right.

Except for the gunfire, way off in the distance, it was a peaceful morning. We all got our shit together and headed east then northeast through the rest of the village—almost like a walk in the park. Some children showed up looking for handouts. I had a Hershey's chocolate bar—the one without the almonds, the one stamped in equal bite sizes—and gave it to the oldest of the five kids surrounding me. He unwrapped the chocolate bar and broke it up, handing each kid a piece until they were gone.

Being on the move again felt strange, but in a good way. I was finally in the shit. I was humping along with my fellow soldiers—a part of a whole with a unit I was a member of. At the same time, I hated the fucking army and the bastards who sent me here. Then thoughts of measuring up, of performing my duties, and of the fucking fanny pack signaling "newbie" crossed my mind. If only I had a rucksack, maybe I wouldn't stand out.

Single file, we moved along a dike between two large rice paddies until we reached a sandy island of palm trees nestled between them and a graveyard off to the northwest. We stopped briefly to see what the plan was from battalion headquarters. I watched the captain in a crouched position with the headset up against his ear. Handing the headset back to Hatfield, he stood up and ordered the lead platoon to advance through the graveyard.

As we inched our way through the sandy graveyard filled with cacti, headstones, and burial mounds, we worked our way toward the rice paddy leading to yet another island. The intermittent gunfire was still off in the distance as we moved north, the mountain range coming closer.

I could see the lead platoon entering the rice paddy, making it thirty feet or so before bursts of gunfire erupted. The first shots came from the island in front of us. Then from off to our left and right. A fucking ambush. Bullets were kicking up everywhere. The gunfire was coming from what appeared to be all directions. The sound, the crack of bullets whistling through the air, set every nerve in my body on edge. A Vietcong fell from the top of a palm tree like in a John Wayne movie . . . guys were screaming, hollering, hugging sand, and looking for cover in the sudden turmoil. Captain Kahele was called for assessments from the lead platoon's lieutenant as he poked his head just above the burial mound to my right. Hershel, a fellow I'd met back in base camp, came running back from the first element with a bloody nose—in fact, no nose, just a bloody mess between his eyes, his nose gone. I looked over at the captain again, and he was barking orders into the radio handset when a bullet pierced his skull, ripping through his forehead. As I continued to look at him, he fell and lay motionless against the sandy mound. His radio operator looked back at me and threw up his hands as if to say, "Now what." The captain was done, motionless. It was up to Lieutenant Turner, the XO, to take over as the next in command. That made me the command radio operator, and I hadn't been in the shit twenty-four hours. I hardly knew how to depress the fucking switch on the handset, let alone perform my duty.

I heard a voice call, *"Texas League six, over."*

"Texas League six, over," the radio speaker repeated.

I yelled into the handset, *"This is Texas League five India, six is down, over."*

The lead platoon lieutenant asked, *"I've got five down in the rice paddy.*

What do we do? Over."

Lieutenant Turner grabbed the handset and responded, *"This is five. Pull back, pull back! Over."*

"Roger that, over."

Three of us hid behind one mound of sand, a grave barely tall enough to shield us. We continued hugging the sand as the graveyard appeared to come alive. The bullets sent grains of sand flying into the air. Like a flock of blackbirds spooked by an evil cat, everyone—in unison—started streaming by. The XO got up first, then Casey, both hunched over as if clearing a low bar, and they ran the best they could back to the island. I hesitated to leave. With the sand crawling with lead, superstition suddenly reared its ugly head, and the thought of "three strikes, you're out" entered my mind. The weight of the radio and all the gear felt awkward. Knowing there were no good options, I got up the best I could and ran. Every step I took seemed to sink me further into the sand; the straps from the pack weighed heavily on my shoulders. If only I could slip out of the pack, maybe I could make it. Running that tape through my mind, I zigzagged as best I could toward the palm trees and the promise of relative safety. Reaching the island and a ridge of dirt just tall enough to hide behind, I started to feel better.

As the remaining guys filtered into the makeshift perimeter, we used our entrenching tools to dig foxholes. I wished for a bigger shovel. I kept digging. There was little to do other than dig. On the second day, the hole I was digging was deep enough you could nearly walk upright. I'd fashioned a sort of staircase on both ends. It felt good to stand up without risking a bullet to the head.

A supply helicopter managed to fly into the southeast end of our perimeter; the captain's request for new underwear, socks, and T-shirts was on it. Sergeant Morgan asked if I wanted them, since no one else wanted to hump the extra weight. Since I'd inherited the captain's rucksack, I replied, "Yeah, I'll take them." Then I started thinking about the old man, the captain that only two days ago had asked how I was doing, assuring me that everything would be all right. I folded the socks, then the T-shirts, and stuffed them into the dead man's rucksack.

The occasional chopper slipped in to resupply our ammo, food, medicine, and whatnot under the strain of gunfire, bullets zinging through the airspace randomly, then relentlessly, followed by an occasional silence. The hope, the pause of relief, the thought: *Perhaps they're gone.* Would we be so lucky? Then it would start anew. A guy on the north perimeter couldn't mentally take it anymore, breaking down to the point we had to evacuate him. It reminded me of Bart from Kentucky back in base camp, the guy motoring around in a cart carrying supplies here and there. He was a former machine gunner; I asked why he wasn't still in the field. He simply said, "I couldn't take it." I found out later he killed some kids in his first firefight, spraying bullets into a stucco house.

Midmorning on the third day, the fire subsided, then nothing. No word of Bravo Company or how they'd withstood the assault. Lieutenant Turner, on orders from Command, ordered us to move out through the graveyard on a sunny day with God clouds floating lightly in the blue sky, with calm sand and headstones.

On approaching the rice paddy holding the remains of the five KIAs, floating in rice water, swollen, we tried carefully to roll and maneuver the bodies onto poncho liners. We feared the flesh—now turned purple—would fall from the bones as we handled them. As we laid them on dry ground, I heard the chopper off in the distance. Then it landed only a few meters away, and we loaded them onto the floor of the chopper and watched as they lifted off into the blue sky.

As we waited for the Hueys to pick us up and deliver us to our next destination, I dreamed of showers, white painted walls, the smell of soap, and driving my '55 Chevy in any direction tethered to nothing other than the open road. I thought of those soon to be zipped up in black body bags and stuffed into refrigerated lockers on the edge of the South China Sea, awaiting destinations they had no control over, their duty at an end. We never said goodbye; we just sat there on the sand in a graveyard with bodies in the air and under our butts.

5

The Bridge

The river running through the city of Bong Son flowed slowly and lazily under the bridge. The foxholes were already dug and fortified with sandbags, so there would be time to reflect on the firefight, the poor bastards in body bags on their way home. I noticed a jeep crossing the bridge with two guys. As they rounded the corner from the bridge, they pulled up next to our foxhole.

"Any you sons of bitches lookin' to get laid?"

"Yeah, sure. Where?"

"Not far," one of them yelled.

I looked over at Casey and Ryan to see if they were up for a little trip. Neither seemed interested. After all, we didn't know shit about these guys. But what the hell, they were wearing army green, and they definitely had round eyes.

"Yeah, I'll go," I said. Then, "Cover for me," I asked Ryan.

The sun was bearing down on our steel pots, but the anticipation was overwhelming. Being able to bust a nut was job one, as the army would say. Christ, they built Sin City just outside of base camp for just such a reason. Out in the field, there ain't no Sin City like back in An Khê, ain't no place for a little relief, so you gotta make good with the locals. All the round-eyes, nurses, candy stripers, and USO womenfolk were reserved for the officer corps. They probably built Sin City so the grunts wouldn't butt fuck each other and lose our will to fight. Who the fuck knows.

It was a damn fine road, even though it was made of dirt. Elevated high between the rice paddies, smooth as a cat's back, the jeep clocking 45 mph. It was a good day.

Just up ahead, I noticed an old man on a bicycle pumping his pedals, going up and down. His whiskers blew in the wind, and he wore one of those conical straw hats strapped to his chin.

Rosco, the fellow riding shotgun, pulled a grenade from his belt, pulled the pin, and heaved it over his head into the bar ditch, where it exploded maybe thirty feet from the old man. As I turned to see what happened, his feet flew off the pedals, the front wheel wobbled, and he fell face-first onto the dirt road with his bicycle tangled in his legs.

Rosco and Jason, the driver, started laughing uncontrollably like it was the best thing ever, as if it was like the Wild West or something.

After the laughter died down, Jason said, "It's payback for the little motherfucker in the hedge line over there." He pointed his finger to the north. "Nearly every time we make this trip, some bastard fires a few shots in our direction. He must be a piss-poor shot 'cause ain't none of us sons of bitches been hit yet."

Fortunately, today, no sniper shots. A good omen for sure as three white stucco buildings emerged up ahead. The buildings surrounded a firepit big enough to cook over. Three young women dressed in black pajamas sat on their haunches around the small burning fire preparing the evening meal, the flames licking up the sides of a black pot hanging from hooks. The largest building could hold maybe ten horny GIs or ARVNs or whoever was in need of a little relief. Flat bamboo benches rested against three walls with a doorway leading to the primary area of operations. Inside there were four beds, two on one side and two on the other, with silk curtains you pulled closed for privacy—almost like a health clinic: you got a problem in need of fixin', these young ladies took care of it. Once the money was paid and the deed was done, the practitioners of love slipped out one after another to an area surrounded by walls now in shadow, walls to keep out the prying eyes of whoever might pass by. I saw a young naked woman holding clothes in one hand, walking to the patio's center, a patio with no roof. She was like a crucible with the sun spilling down on her naked body, illuminating her against the now dark walls: beautiful. She soaked a washrag in the bucket of water and removed the foreign sweat from her breasts, her belly, then she squatted, expelling the fruits of her union. The scene somehow felt like innocence had died a bit as the water rested on the spoiled brick. As I shifted my eyes back to the interior, adjusting to the dark, I noticed the milling about under the roof—shadows buttoning flies, sliding brass-tipped belts through dull brass buckles.

Rosco said it was time to head back.

Energy spent, we rode back down the dirt road. The trip seemed short; before long the bridge lay just ahead.

"Thanks, guys!" I said and jumped out of the jeep. Rosco and Jason disappeared in a cloud of dust then turned onto the bridge. I forgot to look to see if the old man was still in the bar ditch.

Maybe a kid would come by selling those brass bracelets; some called it a friendship bracelet. Perhaps it would bring me luck. Everyone was wearing them.

6

Situation Report

Airlifted somewhere into the Bong Son area, we moved through the barren valley to the base of the mountain range. It was hot, hotter than usual, and the climb up the mountain took its toll. One of my canteens was already empty, and the other half empty. The captain ordered us to sit and rest until a chopper could bring much-needed water. An hour passed as we sat there and looked down from the mountaintop at the empty rice fields lying below, hoping and waiting for the familiar sound of blades slapping the air, all of us down to our last few swigs or none. I couldn't see who it was, but a guy twenty feet away just sort of fell over—passed out. A few minutes later, another one fell over. Still no chopper, no water. Doc had just started tending to one of the poor bastards when the distant sound of a chopper stirred the humid air. With no trees, no shade, the heat would have gotten us all in another hour. I made a mental note: carry more canteens.

On our feet again, following the ridgeline, the noon hour long gone, we found a little cover and a place to set up for the night, dig foxholes, and clean rifles.

Time for a few hands of poker. I was still in the hole thirty bucks to fast Freddie; Beantown native Ryan and New York's own Casey fumbled with their cards, positioning them just so. The four of us enjoyed a brief leisurely moment in time under the cover of our hooch. Interrupting the game, Sergeant Anderson from the 3rd platoon sat down cross-legged at the mouth of the hooch. We didn't know him that well, other than that he was quiet and not particularly friendly.

"Hi, Sarge," Casey said in his thick Yankee accent and laid a card down, calling for a replacement.

The sergeant didn't say a word.

"I'll take two," Freddie said.

I glanced over and saw a grenade in Anderson's right hand.

"Give me four," I said.

None of us did anything out of the ordinary, just continued playing cards. Each of us wondered what was going through Anderson's mind. All of us knew now that the pin was missing from the grenade. His hand was resting on the floor of the hooch. Five minutes passed, and he just sat there with no expression on his face and no words. We continued playing without acknowledging the threat, babbling on as if everything was normal. Then Anderson got up, pushing himself off the ground with his empty hand, and left, not saying a word.

"Damn it, Freddie, I should have called," I said, throwing my winning hand onto the poncho liner, bluffed again. Anderson's legs disappeared from view.

We continued playing, keeping the same tone of voice, happy that Looney Tunes had vacated the premises, all of us in silent acknowledgment that Anderson was up to no good. A couple of minutes later, we heard an explosion. We all figured it for the asshole Anderson, the nutjob adding an extra measure of excitement to our afternoon game. It sounded like he threw the grenade down the hillside where the missing pin probably went earlier. No telling what he was thinking or why he didn't let the handle fly off, giving us about the same amount of time a bull rider gets before being bucked off. Eight seconds and you're either still breathing or gored by a thousand tiny pieces of shrapnel. Why he gave us a pass, no one knows. How do you figure something like that? He just didn't like us for some reason. It happens.

Checking the final numbers—troop strength of the four platoons, the CP, and needed supplies—I pulled out my little book of codes. Finding today's date, I thumbed through the numbers and corresponding letters: Echo Bravo equals two, Charlie Kilo equals three, letters representing numbers, numbers telling stories. Through these codes, the battalion could decipher our situation and needs. Keying the handset, I started my spill, *"Texas league six India, SIT-REP, over."*

"Roger, six India, go ahead, over."

"Roger. Sit-rep line one, Echo Bravo, Charlie Kilo. Line two, Zulu Tango, Mike Foxtrot. Line three, Golf Delta, Alpha Zulu." And so it went as we camped at the crest of the mountain, finishing up with ammo, medical supplies, etc. The sun was hiding behind the sparse trees now, the night creatures waking up, stirring, looking for opportunities. It was time for shift change on the perimeter. I turned over the radios to Ryan for his two-hour shift.

It was time to get back to Harold Robbins's book *The Adventurers*, time to find out what shenanigans Dax and the others were up to in South America. Westerns, adventures, mysteries, love stories, anything to mentally wander off and disappear from this hellhole. I'd brought a copy of *War and Peace* by Tolstoy but left it in my footlocker. All those books I read back in the world—Camus, Kierkegaard, Lao Tzu, Hesse—all them motherfuckers could wait. Ain't no time for thinking and pondering. Every free second, every time the column stopped, every sit-down in the Nam, I'd swing that pack off my shoulder, undo the flap on the rucksack, and grab a bit of Neverland.

Lying down on the air mattress, pulling the poncho liner up over my head, I turned on my trusty angle-head flashlight. You don't want the light sneaking off to enemy eyes. Finding my bookmark, transported back to a revolution in the making, I started reading again—my favorite activity.

I'd just started a new chapter when I heard shouting thirty feet away on the perimeter. With the partial moon and patchy night clouds, the darkness made it hard to see the guys on watch.

One of the newbies with his rifle at the ready shouted, "Halt, who goes there."

Silence.

Again, "Halt, who goes there." You could hear the urgency ratcheting up in his voice.

Silence.

The shadowy figure in front of him stepped back, raised his AK, and squeezed off five rounds; the FNG crumpled to the ground, and the shooter turned and ran down the narrow ridgeline. Before anyone could get their bearings, the gook disappeared into the night.

With the newbie screaming and in shock, Doc ran to his aid. I figured he pumped him full of morphine and started applying tourniquets. The cries subsided, and Ryan called in a medevac.

Thirty minutes later, the familiar sound of chopper blades stirred the air. The medevac was getting close, Ryan in contact with the pilot on his handset. I jumped into the clearing as the light from the medevac searched in the dark, raising my arms and hands like the fellow you see out the window of a jetliner when backing out of a terminal, lowering one hand and then the other until the light from above found me like a deer caught in the headlights. Both arms raised in parallel, hands pointed skyward, I started moving my hands toward me. Following my arm movements, the pilot was on track, and I stretched my arms out level with the ground as he touched down. I'd never done anything like that. I'd never guided in a chopper, never exposed myself to the light. I'd never felt so stupid standing there with my arms raised so

Charlie could focus his iron sights.

But in any case, the newbie was shipped off. Doc said he was lucky: "He was hit in both legs, both arms, and a flesh wound to the abdomen." Point-blank range, and the son of a bitch survived.

I thought to myself, "You got to know when to pull the trigger." Must have been that good-luck brass bracelet he bought back at the bridge that saved his ass.

7

Awards Day

Lined up on a dusty hilltop, dressed in our finest jungle fatigues, we stood in a place I'd never heard of overlooking a small village. Eyes right, dress right dress, at ease, the orders barked out by the sergeant: it was awards day.

Thirty days. Thirty days in the field and now I was being awarded—allowed to wear the infantry rifle with a silver wreath, the Combat Infantry Badge. In the bush, at some point, it would be sewn onto our jungle fatigues with black thread representing the rifle and wreath on a green background. It didn't come cheap, though; ten guys were conspicuously absent from the ceremony. They were excused, dismissed on the battlefield by enemy fire and accidents. They wouldn't be attending any future ceremonies, either, except maybe on Veteran's Day when friends and family drove out to the cemetery to plant a tiny American flag and a splash of flowers, or say a few words over their final resting place. Maybe.

We got not only the badge but a promotion as well. No more PFC; we were specialists now. A single chevron on each sleeve was replaced by black eagles. It seemed odd somehow, the word "specialist." We specialized in shooting M16s and M60s, firing M79s and mortars, setting up claymore mines and trip wires. Searching and destroying. Maybe, with all the fear and mayhem ever present, we'd be special in a different way when we got home, like riding around our hometowns in short yellow buses, having traded our steel pots for plastic helmets.

"Hey, Chris, what're you gonna do with all that extra moola?" I asked as we were dismissed from the formation.

"Save it, I guess. Ain't nothing to buy out here. Ain't like a Sears and Roebuck around every corner."

"You got that right," I said.

As we approached the hamlet at the base of the hill, a middle-aged woman approached Chris and asked if he wanted to "boom-boom."

Chris, one of those guys who carried around a Bible and read scripture every chance he got, accepted the mama-san's offer and disappeared behind a tan house.

Well, there went part of Chris's raise—a wise expenditure, I supposed. Then I started thinking, 10 guys down, 120 guys in our company. Fuck, the math ain't working in my favor. Maybe Chris was right: take whatever pleasure you can 'cause it may be your last. After all, it was biblical: sow your seed, be fruitful, and all—no need to worry about the folks back home. Ain't like anyone was going to know in Pittsburgh, Chris's hometown. The only thing they'd see was the silver-and-blue Combat Infantry Badge and gold eagles worn proudly on his chest and arms. Ribbons, rank, and medals, that's what it's all about.

"How was she?" I asked Chris.

"Great!"

8

Lanny Jr.

As I placed one boot on the skid, turning to position myself on the floor of the copter and leaning against my backpack, we lifted off. Being last to board had its advantages. If it is a hot LZ, either you're the first to be shot or you're the first to escape and find cover. I liked the odds of being on the ground first.

As we flew in formation over the rolling terrain below, I turned my head to get a look at the speed: 90 knots registered on the dashboard. I loved flying. The blades of the helicopter, occasionally chattering from the changing air currents, sounded like music to my ears. Flying beat the hell out of humping through the jungle and villages below.

I could see the lead chopper descending, approaching a grassy hillside, then guys jumping the short distance to the ground, bent over, their heads bowed. You didn't want to get your head lopped off by the blades. When scampering up the hill, the farther you went, the closer to the blades you got; exiting on the downhill side, you might break a leg.

The chopper in front of us started hovering just high enough for its occupants to jump the foot or two to reach land. Standing on the skid now, a hundred and fifty feet from the ground, I grabbed the cutout in the fuselage for balance with my left hand. I had a clear view of the chopper in front of us. A soldier who looked like Lanny—a black kid from Arkansas I'd met on the plane coming from the US—crouched down to clear the blades, made his way up the hill. Then a blast—the blast filled my ears, my muscles tensed up, my hand grabbed on a little tighter. Something wasn't right. Lanny made it only about twenty feet before he fell. The grenade strapped to his ammo belt had exploded, ripping flesh and organs from his knees to his chest, leaving what looked like a shark bite. Somehow the pin on one of his grenades had pulled loose when he jumped off the chopper, giving him his last eight seconds on Planet Earth. How does that happen? Pulling the pin on a grenade takes considerable force. Of course, he realized nothing until the split second when his life came undone. That's what I told myself anyhow.

Our turn. I jumped off the skid and made my way up the hill until I reached the body. I took the attitude of anyone coming across a tragic accident. I had to look. The limbs of the scrub brush acted like a spiderweb, snaring the contents of his wallet along with flesh and blood. I picked up his ID card, then a photo, the usual items. Viewing the snapshot of his family staring back at me with smiling faces felt strange, weird. On inspection, perhaps one of them was his girlfriend or maybe his sister, the tall one a brother for sure, the older ones probably his mom and pop. We were the first to know he wasn't coming home in one piece. Someone soon would be knocking on his parents' door—"We regret to inform." We laid out a poncho liner, rolled what was left of him onto it, and collected what personal items we could find and hoped they'd find their way back to his family.

Finally, a chopper flew in to collect the body. Four of us grabbed the corners of the poncho with Lanny's remains and bent over to clear the rotating danger above, and we loaded him onto the floor.

Time to move out. We made our way to the top of the grassy hill and stopped to rest. Captain Kahele's temporary replacement, Lieutenant

Turner, decided we should eat, since it was near the noon hour. No shade, no trees to lessen the heat. I sat on my butt and pulled a can of apricots from my rucksack. Working the small blade of the P38 around the rim of the can, exposing the contents, I didn't know how to feel. Another man had perished a couple of hours ago, and now it was time to eat. I didn't know how to mourn the passing of yet another fellow soldier, a fellow passenger on the plane coming over here a few months ago, an Arkansan. Or how I was going to forget the faces in the photo staring back at me. I did know one thing: none of us would have traded places.

Dipping the spoon into the tin reminded me: I hated apricots.

9

Captain Carter

A call from Battalion came through the tiny speaker of my handset to say that Bravo Company was in a firefight after walking into an ambush on a steep mountain to the north. Sketchy details were all that came through the earphones. It was "go time," and Captain Carter—after taking over from Lieutenant Turner—was a stand-up guy, like Captain Kahele. Blond and stocky, he was direct in his way of speaking and fair in his approach to the men. Even though he was a newbie, everyone liked him. There wasn't an ounce of bullshit in him. Captain America came to mind. All he lacked was a red, white, and blue shield.

Airlifted to the top of the mountain, we could hear gunfire and grenades exploding below. Of course, we could see nothing from above; the trees and vegetation obscured our view, but the disturbing noises echoing through the trees signaled danger.

"I want to get a closer look and see what the fuck is going on," the captain said to the XO.

"Roger that."

Signaling for Casey, Bobby, and me to saddle up, he ordered, "Let's move out." Then, turning to the XO, he said, "Stay put unless I radio you."

Bobby, the new guy, was worried. He'd grown up in Arizona near the Mexican border. I'd never heard of the town. He probably spent his days chasing lizards and sidewinders through and around century plants and Joshua trees. Until now, he had been easygoing and laid-back; nothing seemed to bother him, not even the occasional scorpion wandering through camp. Accommodating and friendly, he didn't seem to let anything get to him. However, you never know how new guys are going to react when a shitstorm shows up. So, I took an added interest in his mood with what lay before us. I could feel his apprehension as he slung the company net radio onto his back. He followed the captain as we descended into the brush. The captain wasn't depending on someone else's evaluation. He needed to see the situation for himself, and he required communication. It wasn't like he couldn't have sent a platoon down the mountain to evaluate the circumstances; that wasn't his style. He wanted firsthand knowledge. That's what leaders do: make sound decisions based on knowable facts. That's why everyone liked him.

Hanging on to spindly tree trunks, vines, and limbs, we moved closer to the gunfire. Voices in distress started filling our ears, voices calling for help, cries of pain, calling for God's intervention, voices we couldn't reach. The captain stopped in a flat area under the shade of twenty-foot trees and asked Bobby to call the XO. As I looked around, I noticed we were in a perfect bubble of soft light spilling down, seeping through the light green leaves, beautiful but out of step with the gunfire and human cries. From the cocoon, we hatched our next move.

Bobby stammered, "Something's wrong with my radio. It keeps cutting out," as he tried to call the XO.

Annoyed and agitated, the captain asked, "When did you figure that out?"

"I noticed it this morning."

"And you didn't tell anyone?!" the captain said, demanding an answer.

As Bobby remained silent, I switched my radio over to the company frequency and volunteered. "I'll go."

"You and Casey, come with me. Bobby, you stay here. We'll be back."

As the three of us now moved down the steep incline on our butts, the volume from the cries started ratcheting up along with our adrenaline—we were close. The captain told Casey and me to slide over the ridgeline to a safer position.

"I'm going to get a closer look."

"Yes, sir," I said as he slowly moved down, disappearing from view.

Automatic fire erupted, a burst of bullets, the sound, the cracks, the lead projectiles coming our way. Two of them found their mark and ripped through the captain's legs. A short scream and muffled cuss words sent an extra shot of adrenaline through our bodies. I immediately radioed the XO. *"The captain's been hit. We need help, over."* As the captain tried to crawl up to our position, I could hear noise from above crashing through the brush. Armando, Ricky, Emilio, and Ernie passed by us and found the captain not far from our position. They laid out a poncho and rolled the captain over onto it, then, grabbing the corners, they somehow carried him up the steep mountain. Casey and I made our way back to Bobby, and the three of us climbed back to the top. The enemy disengaged for some reason. Maybe they figured their odds were moving in the wrong direction. Who the fuck knows. In the meantime, Bravo Company grabbed their wounded and joined us at the top of the ridge to await evacuation.

Captain America—brave, personable, young, and smart—flew off into the blue sky. I told myself he'd be OK. Heroes never die. At least, not in the comic books.

I checked Bobby's radio when he slipped off to take a shit; it worked just fine. Fucking asshole.

10

Moving Out

After another air assault, another night in Bumfuck, Egypt, Lieutenant Turner took command again until a new captain could be assigned. *Motherfucking gooks shot up my first two captains,* I thought. *What kind of future awaits me . . . or any of us?*

Carefully I pushed another tin of potted meat into a black sock, followed by a tin of peaches. I love peaches. Beans were good too, along with the crackers and pound cake. Then I added some raspberry Kool-Aid to one of my canteens. Mom sent care packages from time to time with various things, but Kool-Aid was special. Fill a canteen from a lazy river; drop in a water purification tablet and a packet of Kool-Aid; when the heat and burning sun scramble your brains under the steel pot, you can find a little comfort taking a swig of flavored river water.

I strapped three socks filled with C rations under the flap of my pack: final preparations for an ambush. Having been on the receiving end of an ambush not too long ago, it was our turn for a change. Of course, there were drawbacks: no nightly helicopter with mail, no Mermite cans full of hot grub, no Korean beer, no nothing from the world for the next three days.

But by God, it was time to catch Charlie with his pants down. Time to get some payback for a change.

Taking a sip from my canteen, I wondered what our actual chances were. Being successful felt strangely remote—pointless, really. It wasn't like the enemy was clueless to our whereabouts. Hell, it was their fucking country, their ground. Besides, a gook told us a while back that we smelled sweet—sweet, sweaty bodies filled with pork and beans, a diet full of sugar and fat. Plus, there was nothing like the whiff of cigarette smoke sifting through the jungle greenery to announce our presence.

I rolled over on all fours to lift the pack and the extra weight to an upright position; it felt heavy with the extra food rations—but doable.

With everyone loaded up and ready, the 1st platoon moved out along the mountainside trail. We were next in line—the command post. One by one, we fell into a rhythm, one boot in front of another. I lit a cigarette and cupped my hand as I took a drag—a habit one got into whether it was day or night. Folks back home wouldn't think a thing about lighting up a cig, holding it between the index and middle fingers, and puffing away. In this world, you held it between the thumb and index finger. If you dared to handle it the way folks did back in the world, ole Charlie would find himself a target right quick. You inhaled, adding oxygen to the burning tobacco, the cigarette tip glowing brighter and brighter, and the little peckerwood in the black pajamas would find his mark.

The triple canopy jungle with every color of green in the book can be beautiful when it shades and hides you from the tropical sun. Of course, it does the same for the enemy. No farther than a couple hundred meters from our camp, my mind started to drift off to my life before the Nam when movement down in the ravine to our lower left registered in my peripheral vision like a shock of electricity. Eyes wide as saucers, I spotted three Cong running, carrying rifles slung over their shoulders, moving at a fast clip. Lester, a machine gunner in front of me, started running, veering off the small trail to the left a bit to get a clear field of fire, trying to keep pace with them. With a belt of fifty rounds or so stretching to the ground, he started firing from the hip, shell casings spitting out, brass littering the jungle hillside—not an easy thing to do with the weight of a machine gun. I was impressed. You've got to be strong to do that. Watching from behind Lester, I thought the scene felt like the TV battle scenes from World War II I used to watch. But unlike in the movies, the speedy figures with bullets kicking up all around them somehow eluded the gunfire and disappeared like magic. Just wasn't their time, I suppose.

I didn't know Lester that well. There are those who hesitate, and there are those who welcome the action. Lester didn't mind mixing it up. When an opportunity presented itself, Lester was there—a man you could count on when the shit started. He wasn't anyone I would have been friends with back in the world: a pockmarked face, eyes a little too far apart, hair a bit too coarse, the bully that ruled the schoolhouse playground. We had little in common, but on this particular day, he was my best buddy. Lester grew up hunting squirrels and critters of every persuasion in a holler in Kentucky, then drafted out of the Appalachian Mountains. Having tried to shoot squirrels out of big ole hickory trees myself back on my grandpa's farm in Iowa, I recognized that the jungle hid these sons of bitches like squirrels—they were always on the wrong side of the tree to get a clean shot, so to speak. They were just as elusive. It was unusual to see them out in the open like that. Lester understood the stakes. And just maybe I was wrong about sneaking up on Charlie. I started thinking that perhaps we just might get some payback after all.

"Hey, Lester, damn good try. I thought you had 'em."

"Me too," Lester said. "Little bastards can run, can't they."

After the brief action, we drifted back into the shuffling rhythm of a single column again.

After an hour or so, something didn't feel right. Reaching down, I noticed a rip in my pants and felt something weird—a funny bump. When we stopped for a breather, I reached down and loosened my bootlaces, un-bloused my pant leg, and discovered bloodsucking leeches—a gaggle of four, tight as ticks. One had even worked its way around to the back of my leg. I worried; maybe one of them had found its way up to my asshole. Can they get inside you? How would you know? You can't feel the little bastards when they're crawling and chowing down. I wondered how these little bloodsuckers found my leg in the first place. Then it dawned on me: those little crawly things trying to keep pace with us were land leeches. I thought they only lived in rice paddies and rivers. I thought wrong.

I was hoping to read a few more pages of my Mickey Spillane novel. But no, I had to get rid of these damn leeches. I pulled the mosquito repellent loose from the elastic band circling my helmet, unscrewed the cap, and squirted the juice on the four bloodsuckers; they dropped to the ground, shrinking up like dried prunes from the formidable assault of a petroleum product. It felt good to ruin their fucking day. Then I noticed a bump on my right leg. How the hell had a little bastard managed to attach itself to my right leg? There were no rips on that pant leg. It seemed everything and everyone wanted to exact its measure of blood in this fuckin' place.

As the day wore on, we came to a clearing, a hole in the canopy. It looked like a bomb had exploded, laying down hundred-foot trees like Tinker toys or fiddlesticks. Entering the hollowed-out space open to the sun's rays, the lieutenant ordered us to make camp. The 1st platoon kept moving, scouting out the area in front of us. With evening closing in, it was time for foxhole digging, hooch building, assigning guard duty, radio watch, the usual shit.

I heard gunfire down in the ravine, not a hundred meters from where we were setting up camp. All of us hunkered down until we could figure out what was happening. After the initial burst of fire, there wasn't any response—no return fire. It occurred to me, and everyone else, that there wasn't much to worry about; maybe Charlie got caught taking a dump.

As it turned out, it was two gooks dressed in their finest black pajamas, a man and a woman. The man, sick with malaria, and the woman, evidently his nurse, from what we could ascertain, were on their way to an underground hospital. The woman was shot dead and left in the ravine; the man, whose arm was nearly blown off, hanging along his side by tendons, flesh, and a little bit of muscle, was brought up to the clearing.

Any hopes of an ambush had been destroyed by gunfire now. I radioed for a medevac to come pick him up, patch him up, and interrogate him. In the meantime, we went through his personal items: his wallet, a photo, and some papers filled with letters none of us understood. Ryan, the inquisitive radio operator, now studying the faces found in the photo, thought the woman staring back at him was the woman lying in the ravine. Maybe it was his wife, he thought, but who knew.

I took pity on the pajama-clad man and offered him a cigarette—a Chesterfield from one of those C ration four-packs. I didn't feel generous enough to offer him a Marlboro. I motioned with my hand, and he acknowledged that he'd like one. So I lit it up and gave it to his only functioning hand. With a slight smile, he took a drag as we waited. After exchanging glances with the man occasionally, I could hear the medevac approaching.

And then, loaded up, the chopper's blades powering up, he was gone.

With darkness approaching, two troopers slipped off down the hillside to the bottom of the ravine and extracted the gold from the dead woman's mouth. I'm not sure how they did it, maybe with the point or the butt of a bayonet. Perhaps the butt of their rifle. She evidently wasn't a practicing member of the betel nut crowd. Otherwise, they'd never know she had gold-filled teeth. A lot of the women chewed betel nut, and the rumor was they did it to discourage foreigners like us from messing with them. Some said they did it to get high. When they smiled, a kind of black moldy substance would obscure their pearly whites.

On radio watch now, I pulled out my P38, unfolded the blade, and pierced the lid of a tin of pork and beans, working the blade back and forth until the lid floated on the juice; then I turned to a tin of crackers. Setting the crackers aside, I punched holes in the cracker tin with my church key. Back in the States, church keys were for opening cans of Oly, short for Olympia, or Coors—and every now and then, to run the point of it down the side of an adversary's car in the high school parking lot. Pinching off some C-4, lighting it with my Zippo, I placed it in the tiny makeshift stove. It was time to heat up my evening meal. Grabbing my mess kit spoon to fish out the floating lid, I took a bite, wishing for some fucking Tabasco sauce; my mood dampened as the flavorless meal reached my gut.

Morning came soon enough. Again we packed up and headed out to who knows where. The point man started moving to the west into the jungle, melting into the greenery, the land of hundred-foot trees, the leeches trying to keep pace, all of us in tow—like a string pulling tight. The demons of war packed in the belly of our column; a dead gook's gold stuffed into the pockets of our souls.

11

Her Charge

The little girl stood on the south side of the circular rice paddy, maybe fifteen feet from the edge, tending to a water buffalo grazing just a short distance from her bare feet. I figured she was about ten years old, but oddly enough, her hair wasn't black, more like dishwater blond—probably due to cross-pollination with the French. Ten years ago—that would make it about the time the French got their asses kicked at Dien Bien Phu. It was a pastoral scene, beautiful, a child shepherding her charge, plenty of vegetation to eat. It was amazing how a little kid could push around these huge animals like it was nothing, no fear.

As intruders, we pierced the serenity, disturbed the peace, and shuffled our way around the edge of the rice paddy under the shade of trees; I kept an eye on the buffalo. They were big and aggressive. Given our past experiences, I was reasonably sure they were prejudiced against round eyes. Some thought it might be due to our diet, our fatigues drenched in sweet sweat, cigarette smoke, smelly armpits; maybe the English language irritated them. Who knows?

Fifty meters from where I first spotted the beast, the son of a bitch took a distinct disliking to us and charged. Mud flipping up, nostrils flared, the creature reached full speed in nothing flat and was coming straight at me. Four of us opened up with our M16s on full auto. The bullets ripped into his hide but didn't stagger him; he just kept charging. My ass cheeks were so tight, I wouldn't shit for a month.

The bastard finally fell ten feet in front of us. The adrenaline was coursing through our bodies in overdrive. Having escaped disembowelment, I stared at the carcass a few seconds then searched for the little girl. She was in the line of fire not far away. She appeared to be fine standing there. She hadn't moved an inch, no expression on her face—a stoic response from such a small child. She had to be beyond scared. She must have wanted to run away. But she just stood there. Perhaps she'd been schooled not to run from us. Maybe she thought she'd end up like the dumb animal at our feet.

I replaced the spent magazine with a new one and pulled the bolt back, chambering a round. Luckily, the damn thing didn't jam. Looking over at Casey, I said, "Close one, huh?"

"No shit, Sherlock!" he responded.

With the image of the little girl tending her charge and the beautiful landscape, the moment curiously out of step with the rifle in my hands, I heard the words, "Move out," from the head of the column.

12

LZ English

Doc looked into one eye, then the other, using his thumb and index finger, holding the eyelids apart.

"You got something going on in there, and it doesn't look good," Doc said.

"My head is killing me, Doc, and my neck hurts like hell," I said.

Doc leaned back, rested his hands on his medical pouches. "You need to get tested. I'm sending you to LZ English. Maybe they can figure out what's going on."

Even with my head and neck pounding, I thought to myself, *At least I'm getting out of the field for a few days.* Hopping on a chopper, I raised my hand a bit to acknowledge my comrades as the helicopter lifted into the clear blue sky. The clinic—LZ English, in the Bong Son area—the hustle and bustle of one of our biggest bases, was only a few minutes away by air.

"Could be hepatitis," the doc at the clinic said. "The whites of your eyes look a little yellowish. We may have to ship you back to base camp. We'll see, maybe tomorrow, if you aren't any better." He continued his examination then had his assistant assign me to a cot in the green canvas-covered clinic. "We'll take a look at you tomorrow," he said as he moved on to the next patient.

"Hepatitis, fuck, what the hell is that? Sounds bad," I said to the poor bastard in the bunk next to me. "I mean, it's better than being shot, but what the fuck?"

No response.

As I lay down on my cot, the fellow with a rash on his leg asked, "Hey, you want to see a movie tonight?"

Here I was, all fucked up in the head with worry, and he wanted to go to a fucking movie. Then I thought, what the hell. "Movies, they show movies here?" I asked.

"Sure do. I think they're showing *Born Free* tonight."

"*Born Free*, wow, that's weird." Like any of us are born free. I sure the fuck wasn't free, not since that goddamn letter showed up in my mailbox ordering my ass off to war. Ain't no freedom in that. And this wasn't no WWII when the Japs bombed Pearl Harbor, and we had something to fight for. "Born Free," my ass.

"Yeah, I'll go," I said.

An amphitheater served as the movie house; the afternoon light had turned dark, so now the movie would show up on the small white canvas screen. There was no concern for the level of sound as the opening music played loudly in my ears. It was a nice, comfortable night with all the beer we wanted only a few steps away. It wasn't like out in the field where you and a hundred other pissed-off motherfuckers had to share five cases of warm Korean beer.

The movie ended with the title tune stamped in my memory. "Born Free, free as the wind blows . . ." the theme song went. A catchy tune, for sure. The sergeant in charge of us sick bastards ordered us to stand guard at one of the perimeter bunkers. Rash Baby Eric, Stomach Flu Jonathon, and I headed out to the bunkers with rifles in tow.

"Fucking asshole," Rash Baby said.

"You got that right," Jonathon chimed in.

"Here we are, sicker than shit," Rash Baby continued, "and the fucking army can't come up with some able-bodied sons of bitches to man their fucking perimeter. Fucking rear echelon assholes."

It had been dark for a couple of hours now, and having relieved the guys manning the bunker, we were in a sour mood and pissed that they'd assigned us to guard duty. Rash Baby came up with an idea. "I know we're fucked up on beer and don't deserve this shit being sick and all, but how about we pull the pins and toss all these grenades just for the hell of it?"

"Sounds like a plan," I said, with my flashlight's dim light reflecting off the bunker's roof.

We crawled up onto the roof, having gathered all the munitions we could find.

"Looks like fifteen or twenty grenades, five or six smokes, and a few illumination rounds," Stomach Flu Jonathon figured.

Rash Baby picked up a grenade, pulled the pin, and heaved it out into the night. *Kaboom!* Then I did the same. *Kaboom!* Then all three of us started pulling pins and chucking them as fast as we could. Like it was the Fourth of July, I slammed down an illumination round, launching it high into the air, where it exploded, casting light down on invisible enemy soldiers.

"What's going on? Are we under attack?" said a nervous voice coming from the bunker next to us. We didn't answer; we just kept firing off what was left of the flares and grenades. After squeezing off a few rounds from my M16, we decided to call it a night. Jonathon, Rash Baby, and I climbed down from the roof of the bunker to sleep in comfort behind four walls made of sandbags and steel supports. Scrunching up my poncho liner to use as a pillow, I asked Rash Baby, "Think anyone will come a-knockin'?"

"Would you?" Rash Baby said with closed eyes.

13

Binh Dinh Province

Rejoining my guys after a week in sick bay, I was almost happy to see the poor bastards. The 616th hospital in An Khê was fine and dandy, but I was bored—not that being tended to by round-eyed female nurses wasn't a benefit, but there was nothing to do but wait for a positive test report for hepatitis. What that would have meant, I don't know. But, after a week of finger pricks morning and night, I was ready to get my ass out of there. Doc finally released me to return to the field.

Flying in on the supply Huey, I spotted my guys digging on top of a bald hilltop. There were smiles all around as I approached. It was bunker digging time.

Ryan looked up from the pit, the sweat shining off his bare shoulders, and asked, "How're you doing, man?"

"Oh, I've been better; guess I'm OK, though. The docs never did find out what was fucking me up. I'm guessing that's a good thing."

Surveying the surroundings, I added, "Looks like some downtime for a change. Bunker duty."

As Ryan shoveled another scoop of dirt out of the shallow pit, he said, "Yeah, fucking entrenching tools suck."

Casey, standing to my left in his trousers and boots, said, "Beats humping the bush."

Everyone was silent, watching Ryan jamming the blade into the dirt, a pause in the usual insults. With Ryan in the pit, it was our job to fuck with him by turning insults into anger, anger into digging.

Then word came to move out. Move out before the sun reached high noon. To where?

One minute you were cooling your heels on a barren hill in Binh Dinh Province, digging foxholes and bunkers, enjoying an excellent field of fire—thinking there ain't no one gonna sneak up on you. Then it was time to pack your bags and fly off to who knows where. In no time, we found ourselves back in An Khê waiting to board a C-130 headed for Dak To—the 173rd Airborne base camp. The rumor was, them poor bastards got a couple of companies fucked up by uniformed NVA—no black-pajama motherfuckers out there close to the Cambodian-Laotian border.

"Someone said the NVA cut their heads off, decapitated those airborne sons of bitches," Ryan said.

"That's fucked up, man," I said.

Two runways big enough to allow C-130s to land were clear for our arrival. The rumors reverberated, bouncing about off the walls of the fuselage and swimming around in our heads: of headless airborne soldiers, being overrun on the Ho Chi Minh Trail. Deplaning and looking around in all directions, we saw nothing but mountains. Someone said the battle took place south of here.

It appeared that they didn't have much of a perimeter, yet C-130s were flying in and out. The local natives—tall, dark, and slender, and the women bare-breasted—walked through the camp carrying shit without a hint of concern from the grunts stationed here. That may have been standard operating procedure for the 173rd, but the first thing we did was set up a perimeter—no tribal folks wandering through willy-nilly.

A story was circulating about as we settled in for the night that one of the airborne guys raped one of those bare-breasted native girls. He thought he'd gotten away with it unscathed until one night, one of the locals slipped through the perimeter in the middle of the night, sliced off his Johnson, and slipped out without capture. I guess the local tribesmen believed in that old biblical adage: an eye for an eye.

It was time to blow up air mattresses, eat some C rations, and get some shut-eye, 'cause there was no telling what the morning would bring.

14

Dak To

We ventured out west a few klicks to get a feel for the terrain. Get our feet wet, you might say. Resting on a hilltop, twisting the cap off my canteen, I could see a lone chopper approaching.

"Looks like we have a visitor—maybe the new captain," I said to Roger. "Don't know much about him. He's supposed to be a West Pointer, from what I hear."

Captain Gary Lawrence got off the chopper, all puffed up like a toad in heat. New meat. He approached us like he was some sort of MacArthur, like this was the beach in the Philippines in those newsreels, and he'd come to rescue us poor bastards. The only thing missing was a corncob pipe. To look at him, just maybe, he had it stuck up his ass.

"Where's the lieutenant in charge, soldier?" he asked.

"I'll get him, sir," I responded.

His attitude was all wrong. Just the way he asked me to get the lieutenant pissed me off—definitely a rear echelon type, a by-the-book kind of an asshole. I didn't trust him from the get-go; he acted like it was all about him and his career, and we were the pawns he needed to achieve position and stature.

After he and the lieutenant exchanged greetings, it didn't take long to prove my assessment. "Get the colonel on the horn," he ordered. I handed him the handset to command. After some chatter, Lawrence bent down on one knee, laid a map on the ground, and started finding coordinates, moving his index finger from one point to another, double-checking the latitude and longitude.

"*Roger, one zero, Texas League six, over and out,*" said the captain. He then handed me the handset to Battalion. and grabbed the company net, depressing the button on the handset. "*This is six, we're moving out in thirty minutes, over.*"

Saddled up, moving down the hillside—the undergrowth was thick—I pulled out my machete and started hacking. I could see the guys ahead of me hacking too, cutting and moving down the hillside.

After a couple of hours, finally stopping for a little rest, the captain pulled out his map, checking, running his finger over it again, looking at his compass, shooting glances in one direction then the other. He was noticeably irritated by our lack of progress. It was like the motherfucker couldn't read a map. Either that, or he had shit for brains. I didn't know a lot about maps, but I could damn sure read contour lines. With vines and brush everywhere, the Nam ain't no fuckin' football field, flat as a pancake. There ain't no flat land like back in Tigerland, or wherever he trained.

The captain grabbed the frame of his rucksack, slipping his arm under one of the straps, and slung it onto his back. Almost ignoring the mood of the rest of us, he flashed a glancing look in my direction. "Get moving, soldier!" he ordered.

Fucking vines caught in the flash suppressor, the antenna hanging up, fucking sweat running down the crack of my ass. The old man pushed us, stopping only to check our progress on the fucking map with its tight little contour lines; the only thing tighter was those bloodsucking land leeches.

"We're behind schedule," the captain murmured to himself.

Pissed off about not reaching the agreed-upon destination, the captain ordered us to set up camp, dig foxholes, and set out claymores and a couple of listening posts beyond the perimeter. Darkness started raising its ugly head, the hour getting late. There was no time to dig our foxholes, only the captain's; making noise after dark wasn't an option.

Morning broke, and with a short hike to a flat area so choppers could pick us up, we were on our way back to base. Chalk off another search-and-destroy mission, just a long hike in the jungle led by a wannabe, tight-assed captain.

The first sortie of choppers slowly emerged in the early afternoon sky, then landed in the usual formation with the blades still spinning. My steel helmet firmly in place, grenades and ammo hooked into my belt and straps, holding the M16 at the halfway point, balanced in my right hand, I lowered my head, timing my approach to one of the choppers.

From high over the jungle floor below, I could see an opening. Looking down as we passed overhead, I saw structures, unique structures with roofs shaped like praying hands pointing up to the sky. Must be the village where those natives lived. Fascinating. Then they were gone.

As near as I could tell, it was thirty minutes or so before I spotted a hole in the canopy 500 feet below. I thought to myself, *Holy shit, this doesn't look good.* Just enough trees knocked down to squeeze in some Hueys. Again, I thought, *Whose fucking idea was this, anyhow?* The hole in the canopy got closer as we descended; how would I avoid landing on a stump or a log? Fuck it; I jumped from the helicopter's skid as it hovered three feet off the ground. The uneven terrain made it hard to keep my balance with all the shit in my pack.

Heading what felt like north as best I could, I had difficulty navigating around and over the downed trees. Finding a place to anchor my butt,

I waited for the second sortie.

With everyone on the ground now, we started moving to the north, everything and everyone locking into place. Tall, beautiful trees surrounded us—hundred-foot-tall trees, maybe taller, forty-foot trees, and of course the thick leafy bushes and vines. A welcome canopy to hide us from the searing sun.

No more than a hundred meters from the landing zone, we found evidence of human activity: a trail. Not just any trail, but a damn fine one, with reinforced wooden steps and landings wide enough to sit in small groups to reorder your loads, gather your thoughts, rest up. Not only was it one fine trail—as it ran up and down the mountain—it looked well-traveled and owned by folks not partial to our presence. We were not alone.

Moving single file, making it to the top of one hill, then another, we finally set up a perimeter. I had an uneasy feeling in the pit of my stomach. The fancy trail had to be a part of the Ho Chi Minh superhighway. And those NVA that took out the 173rd, cutting off heads, dressed in their Sunday best uniforms, probably traveled down this very path. We were like unsuspecting mice; I imagined cats with tails hung low moving just beyond our senses, a step at a time, waiting. I could almost see them licking their chops—another battle on their turf, on their terms.

Setting up radio watch, tying bamboo poles together—too late to dig foxholes—it felt like we were waiting for the unleashing of holy hell. I started worrying about how the hell we were going to get out of here since it had been so hard to get in. And where was the artillery support? Geez, we'd flown a long fucking way.

No defensive artillery rounds that night. The forward observer sat on his thumbs with nobody to call. The 105mm guns back in Dak To couldn't reach us.

"We're fucking bait, man, slung out here without a fucking fishing line to reel us in," I said.

Private First Class Robert Shores, Specialist Thomas Bourne, First Lieutenant Duncan Jeffery, PFC Kenneth Wright, PFC Walter Locke, and I sat in a circle. "This is fucked up," Robert said softly. Uncharted territory, that's where we were.

Robert had grown up in Minnesota, liked to fish for walleye—beautiful fucking lake fish, according to him—in the Land of 10,000 Lakes. He said nothing tastes better than a walleye. He talked about ice fishing on frozen lakes, eating cheap hamburgers at the local White Castle burger joint. I don't think there was a mean bone in his body—he was a polite, well-mannered Lutheran boy. His mother—worried about his prospects in the Nam—bought him a chrome-plated 38mm Smith & Wesson revolver for extra protection.

"Yeah, I know what you mean," Lieutenant Jeffery chimed in finally.

"What do you think our chances are?" Thomas asked, looking down at the knife in his hand, digging at nothing in particular.

"I don't know, man, not good. This fucking place really freaks me out," Robert said after taking another drag on his cigarette, the smoke spiraling up between the thumb and index finger of his cupped hand. Sometimes he'd blow smoke rings, holding his mouth just so, but not this time.

"Come on, guys; it'll be all right," I said, trying to cheer them up, trying to change the mood. The lieutenant didn't say a word, just looked out into the jungle, deep in thought.

They usually talked about home, what they'd do when they got there, their girlfriends, shit like that, but not tonight.

"What was that little town you're from?" I asked Robert.

No response.

"Have you heard from your girlfriend?"

"Not for three weeks now," he said. Then he was lost in thought again. He'd shown me a picture of her a while back—a real knockout, with a pretty smile, long blond hair flipping up at the shoulders. It looked like a high school senior photograph.

The mood was still laden with worry and what-ifs that this might be our last merry-go-round. There weren't no Dale Evans and Roy Rogers singing "Happy Trails" playing through our minds; it was more like "Blowin' in the Wind" by Bob Dylan.

Morning came, and it was time to get moving. The captain ordered the 2nd platoon to scout out the trail leading down the hill—there had been no time the night before for such folly. By the time the point man reached the bottom of the ravine with all thirty guys evenly spaced a few meters apart, bullets started ripping through the air from their right. AK-47s for sure. A fucking ambush, just like the one back in Bong Son. We had no fucking clue, just like before, how the little bastards had anticipated our first move correctly. What the hell were we thinking? Or better yet, what the hell was the captain thinking? Don't take the side road through the woods out of Dodge; no, take the goddamn fucking highway like it was a Sunday drive. Guys started hugging the earth with no cover, fumbling with their M16s, firing back meager bursts. You could hear 'em, you couldn't see 'em; it wasn't like they didn't know we were in the neighborhood, choppers coming from the east the day before breaking the normal rhythms of jungle sounds. Chopper blades slicing, chattering through the tranquility, announcing our arrival.

"Everybody line up; we're going to flank the bastards," yelled the captain.

I looked over at Robert, his M16 at the ready. Thomas was a bit farther away.

"Move out!" the captain ordered.

At the top of the ridge, Robert, slowly putting one foot in front of the other, a bit ahead of me, raised his rifle and fired a burst. I couldn't see what he was shooting at, but with a voice of excitement he blurted out, "Got the motherfucker—he didn't even see me." Then Tom opened up on my right. With no bullets flying up the hill, it was an unexpected maneuver, for sure. "Hey, man, I got me a trophy, man, a fucking AK. Going to tag that son of a bitch for home," said an exuberant Robert.

When the fire trickled to a halt, Thomas managed to grab a souvenir AK too. We were smiling like Cheshire Cats, trophies in hand, the dust settled, the 2nd platoon reporting no casualties. The flanking maneuver worked beautifully. Everyone was whole and intact. I thought it was a fucking miracle of biblical proportions. It was a great day so far, and we'd barely started.

Maybe the asshole captain did learn something back at West Point. By the time we got everything tagged, trophies secured, it was lunchtime.

Most everyone was looking forward to getting some more payback. We saddled up and moved north down from the crown of our temporary base, leaving the ready-made trails to the NVA. The underbrush wasn't bad, the leaves competing for sunlight a hundred feet up, beautifully shading us as we moved up and down the terrain pumped with anticipation and enthusiasm.

As the hours passed, I started to become concerned; it was getting late. I started thinking it was time to head back to our old perimeter. I didn't want to be stuck in the bush with what little supplies we'd brought with us. Like last week when we had humped all day up and down mountains with so little time left, we couldn't dig foxholes. Oh, we had time to dig the captain's foxhole, but not ours. That still pisses me off. When darkness comes, the sound of entrenching tools wailing away, echoing through the night air, will alert all the evil critters of your whereabouts.

All afternoon, we'd not found anything remotely resembling the enemy, unless you want to count the occasional tiger claw marks on a tree here and there.

Pushing our way farther from our base, with sundown not far off, we started moving up a fairly steep hill. The point man was nearing the top when gunfire, machine gun fire, echoed through the leaves and branches, and then screams and moans. More machine gun fire, then M16 return fire. More screams. Sounds of two, maybe three guys hit, judging from the tone and pitch, the lead guys, not thirty meters in front of me, down. And it was more than one machine gun, maybe two. Heads covered with steel pots bobbed up and down, crouched over, weaved back and forth, scurried down the hillside toward me. The weather turned sour with a misty rain. Those who could backtracked out of range to a safe distance, to where the captain and others had stopped. No one knew what to do, not even the captain. With the sounds of the wounded adding pressure to the situation, the captain called his lieutenants for a powwow. The captain's decision was to have the 2nd platoon flank the machine guns—a decision Lieutenant Hamilton strongly disagreed with. He and his platoon were to move higher up the mountain ridge until they were perpendicular to the bastards, then move down, flanking them from their left as we had done earlier. Hamilton figured it was a suicide mission and made his objections known. He walked lethargically back to give the news to his men.

Sitting on a fallen tree with his men gathered around him, not forty feet away, Hamilton took a bullet between the eyes. His head snapped back then forward, his body falling to the jungle floor, covered in fallen leaves. Because he had been so angry with the captain's decision on tactics, he'd paid little attention to his own safety and paid the ultimate price. That bullet had Lieutenant Hamilton's name on it. Take out command and communication; that's the name of the game—a single rifle shot.

Freddie, the RTO pressed the button on the handset and called six: "*Lieutenant Hamilton is down, over.*"

"*Roger that. Who is this, over?*"

"*Freddie, sir, over.*"

"*Put the staff sergeant on the horn,*" barked the captain into the handset.

"*Yes, sir.*"

"*This is Nelson, over.*"

"*You're in charge, and I want you to take the high ground and flank them bastards, over.*"

"*Roger that.*"

Sergeant Nelson, a big, confident soldier, started getting the platoon organized and moving slowly to the right and up the hill above the machine gun's position—just far enough to be out of sight.

There were at least two of them, but the force against us was unknown. How many there were, who knew? Where had that stray bullet come from, the one that took out Lieutenant Hamilton? There were lots of unanswered questions. With Lieutenant Hamilton lying crumpled on the ground a few meters away, Staff Sergeant Nelson didn't question the captain's order; he just reacted. In position now, Sergeant Nelson ordered the platoon to advance toward the enemy position, hoping for another surprise.

More gunfire. Listening to Freddie—Sergeant Nelson's radio operator—on the handset, I heard him say into the mike, "*Robert's down, Minnesota's been hit, over.*"

"*Roger that, over,*" I said, and handed the handset to the captain.

The captain looked confused. His eyes were darting about, calculating—2nd platoon was in deep shit, with conditions growing worse. The night was falling; we had no artillery. Was an air strike even possible with these clouds? All kinds of shit was going through his head. I could see it. Then, as the last option, he called for everyone to line up for a frontal assault. Still lying low, I pondered the captain's decision. What kind of an answer was that? No one was in reserve. We had no support. Daylight was fading fast, the wounded lying in front of us, and to our right, more cries and moans were still echoing through the gunfire. The rest of the company, now moving into position, all lined up below the bastards dug in above.

The captain's order surprised me somehow as he yelled in a loud and forceful voice, "Charge!" With glory or not written all over his face, by God, we were going.

In the dimming light, the captain and two others, flanking him right and left, obeying his order, started running up the hill, crouched over, rifles at the ready, getting smaller. The rest of us didn't make a move. With the captain a few steps in the lead, thirty meters closer to the enemy, shots rang out, ending the captain's quest to conquer the hill and save the day. With the captain hit, lying facedown from what I could tell from my position, the other two, unharmed, lay beside him. José Gonzales, to his right, yelled down the hill, "The captain's hit! He ain't movin'." José and Jason, lying on either side, contemplated their next move. Suddenly, the gunfire subsided to nothing. The little cocksuckers *di di'd*, figuring it was time to vacate the area. José and Jason grabbed the captain by the arms and dragged him down the hill to where we were. Seventy meters from the point of contact, Mason, the captain's radio operator (who had also failed to heed the captain's order to charge), went through his pack looking for whatever personal items we might be able to send back home.

"This is fucked up, man," Mason said. "Too bad. He wasn't such a bad guy, was he?" he continued.

"Yeah, right. If that sum-bitch were on fire, I wouldn't cross the road to piss on him," Tex, from the 3rd platoon, said. "Can you tell if the SOB took the bullet in the chest or back?"

"Can't tell," Mason said.

It reminded me of the old story about the Indian chief ordering his braves into battle and ending up with arrows in his back. If your braves think you're full of shit, chances are fifty-fifty you can get it from both directions.

The mortar platoon was now looking for a gap in the canopy, an opening big enough for a chopper to lower a stretcher. We needed to evacuate our wounded. The platoon found one about a football field away, down one hill and up another. It was a steep climb. The rain continued to fall. The mortar platoon lieutenant called in coordinates. The rest of us answered the orders from Lieutenant Nelson—the newly crowned company commander. I liked him, a no-nonsense guy like Captain Carter. He knew how to treat his troops. None of the textbook shit. Tall, with a muscular build and close-cropped hair on the sides with an unruly clump jutting out over his forehead, he made sound judgments based on experience without the arrogance of the newly deceased captain.

I grabbed one end of a poncho liner along with three others. Robert lay between us, barely breathing, gut-shot. The big grin I saw earlier when he was carrying that AK had turned to a grimace, pain replacing pleasure, the treasured trophy a distant memory. As it continued to rain, the jungle floor turned soggy and slick, the tread on our boots useless. It became harder to keep my balance. Halfway up the hill to the opening, my footing gave way, and I slid down the steep hillside. The other three managed the best they could. I clawed my way back to them and tended my corner of the poncho liner. I could hear the copter approaching, the sound reaching us through the rain and black sky. Robert was hardly making noise now, a moan here and there.

Illumination rounds fired into the sky, signaling the medevac of our whereabouts, yellow smoke billowing up from the canister on the muddy ground, swirling, mixing with the rain, the men milling about.

Finally, we reached the top of the hill and the opening. The medevac's light shone down through the opening of the canopy, shadows from trees moving across dead, wet leaves, the light making them sparkle as they moved about from the force of wind overhead. We lowered Robert down onto the damp ground. From the arm attached to the copter, a gurney swung back and forth, coming closer. Robert's mouth opened, a gasp for air, then nothing. The need for speed was gone. So close.

"Anyone see his Smith and Wesson?" Freddie asked lamely.

We picked Robert up again and laid him down next to the captain, Lieutenant Hamilton, and the others with ponchos pulled up over their heads, exposing their motionless boots, rifle bayonets piercing the earth, helmets resting on rifle butts. We waited for the chaplain. The chopper, with our wounded aboard, was now gone.

A few days later, on a jungle trail leading up and down the twisting terrain, I followed Lieutenant Nelson. I was behind him when we stumbled onto a corpse lying in a tight turn of the small trail. It was a gook barely there, dressed in a faded uniform like a child in his daddy's suit. Bones were sticking out of the sleeves and pants with just enough flesh left that the maggots were having trouble finding the last bits of rotten flesh. They'd already polished off the head. The maggots, the size of dung beetles, were almost frantic, scrambling about; there were so many that the clean white bones were barely visible. His bony right hand lay only inches from his AK-47; the lieutenant picked it up and pulled the trigger, firing every 39mm round in the magazine. Judging from the body's condition, it must have been lying there for maybe thirty days or so. Since the lieutenant's M16 kept jamming on him, he traded his Colt in on an AK. He figured, if we're here to kill, he'd better have something that will do the job.

After we made it back to Dak To on a July morning, a thin blanket of security started to sink in. The sheer number of troops on base gave us all a bit of comfort. Some downtime was in order. On our way back, we happened to cross a river and lingered long enough to take a bath of sorts. I couldn't remember the last time I had a bath. It had been months.

With nighttime approaching, it was time to send out a small long-range patrol to the mountains to our north. They were to position themselves above any trails leading out of the ravine and alert us of any enemy forces who might have the idea of coming for a surprise visit.

"If you hear any movement, don't engage. Key the handset twice," the lieutenant told them. "We'll be monitoring and will respond accordingly."

"Yes, sir."

Zero two hundred hours, and Casey woke me up for my watch.

"Anything going on?"

"Nope."

I was having trouble staying awake. Then I thought about the guys lying on the mountainside above a mountain trail. The only thread to their salvation, should a shitstorm start, was the static the speaker makes when you key the handset. On the hour, one static beep, everything cool, and you'd return the beep. Two static beeps meant they were in a world of shit.

15

Kontum

With my hand in the cutout of the Huey, I stepped out onto the skid.

"What're you doing, man?" Casey asked.

Looking out at the mountain ahead of us, I turned my head and answered, "Getting a better look."

"You crazy motherfucker. It's a thousand feet to the ground," he yelled back.

I didn't care. Ninety knots registering to the instrument panel, the mountaintop fast approaching, the ground coming closer and closer. I felt free. The chopper slowed, hovering just above the ground, and I stepped off the skid onto a barren spot of land; a cornfield lay a short distance away, the green stalks aligned in perfect rows. With the chopper rising into the air behind me, I entered the field, breaking off an ear, peeling the husks away, exposing the yellow corn; I took a bite. The kernels jarred my teeth. They were hard, tasting like caulk. The image of steaming hot corn on the cob, slathered up with real butter, sprinkled with salt, fresh from my grandpa's garden, vanished. I tossed the ear to the ground.

"You're a fucking idiot," Casey said. "You can't eat raw corn."

"What the fuck do you know about farming? You're from New York

City."

"I may be, but I ain't no fucking idiot," he said with a smile. He had me there.

There was no evidence of a farmer in the area, no houses, sheds, tools, no nothing, only the cornfield. We were in the middle of nowhere, surrounded by mountains in all directions, yet someone was tending the field—so many mysteries.

Still pissed about the corn, I flashed to memories of summer vacations on my grandpa's farm: hickory trees infested with marauding, thieving squirrels, the suspension bridge separating the farmhouse from the barn, stuffing firecrackers into corn cobs, lighting them, and throwing them at my brothers. Great fun. And ghost stories told in the darkness of an upstairs bedroom. Today, it was raw corn and grenades—no childhood pretending here.

The weather was tolerable for a change, high on a mountaintop: none of the rainy shit, just blue skies and decent temperatures. It felt safe, oddly enough. Beautiful surroundings were a welcome change after Dak To, where the tentacles of triple canopy had choked the life out of the captain and the others. My mood changed as we humped down the mountainside, melting into the greenery, grunts sliding in and out of view, the valley still a couple of klicks away. The heat and humidity lay in wait, sweat soaking my fatigues, the trees holding the moisture in like a sweaty sheet, no breeze. The straps of the pack, the radio, the weight of all my shit dug into my shoulders, pissing me off even more: fuck this place. Fuck this army, fuck everyone and everything. We finally broke loose from the jungle onto the canyon floor.

Emerging in front of us was an actual road, a winding, somewhat flat dirt road at the convergence of two mountain ranges, stretching far out in front of us, first weaving, then straightening. There was an occasional house here and there as we moved along. The city of Kontum lay off in the distance, and on our right, an airfield—a small air force installation—revealed itself. Not far from the hangar, at a small table next to the runway, sat two airmen. They looked in our direction briefly with drinks cradled in their hands, taking occasional sips. I wondered what they thought of a long line of grunts, who hadn't seen anything resembling a town in months, who hadn't bathed in months. The closest thing to a bath was wading through a river. They had no idea where we'd been. The scene of them lounging in their chairs pissed me off for some reason. Here they were enjoying the afternoon, sipping adult beverages in relative safety, discussing who knows what. It wasn't fair. We were the underbelly, the scary ones, the ones you cross to the other side of the road for if you see us coming.

On the outskirts of town, we set up a perimeter and took the afternoon off to enjoy whatever the city had to offer, the corn a distant memory. A young blond girl on a Vespa scooter rode by heading south out of town. Perhaps a French girl on her way back to a rubber plantation. Maybe a mirage, I thought. It was odd, out of place—remnants of French folks still living here even after their army got walloped. Not everyone went home, obviously. How do you manage that when the host rejects a foreign infection? Guess the piaster speaks louder than the gun.

Stores lined both sides of the street; motorbikes bellowing out gray two-cycle exhaust raced by, mixing with the pedestrian traffic reminiscent of Bong Son. Casey, Freddie, Ryan, and I found a small table with four chairs outside a restaurant like you'd see in a James Bond movie. It was a small, wobbly metal table hardly big enough to set four plates on. But food wasn't what we were interested in.

Holding up four fingers, I asked the pretty young girl as she approached, "Four beers, please." I didn't specify the brand. A couple of minutes later, she came out of the pink stucco restaurant with a platter of four bottles of tiger 33 beer—a blue label with tiger spelled out in English—and four glasses filled with ice.

"Warm beer over ice; what's up with that?" I asked.

I poured the beer into the ice-filled glass. Even though Tiger 33 sucks, at least it was cold and alcoholic.

I took a swig and placed my beer on the small, rickety table. Ryan downed the last bit of ice in his glass and looked my way.

"Four more?"

"Hell yeah!"

Casey looked around as if searching for something, "This is nice and all, but I think we need a little female action."

"Well, we ain't gonna find it here," I said. "I think we need to look for another kind of establishment, the kind that would satisfy our horizontal appetite." On the outskirts of the central district was a tan building with four lovely young ladies sitting on bamboo chairs. Looking in our direction, they hollered in broken English for us to join them.

"You want boom-boom, GI?"

"No, no," Ryan protested. He was married and made it known he was remaining faithful to his wife back in Boston.

"Maybe," I answered the young lady.

Casey, turning to me, said, "This ain't no Sin City, but it'll do." He was the only one of us who'd had the pleasure of visiting Sin City. Sin City: a dozen bars named after states back in the good ole US of A. It had a horseshoe-style layout, built by the Army Corps of Engineers just outside the base perimeter in An Khê. A symbiotic relationship. The girls picked up a little cash, and the soldiers uncorked the sperm bank. As an introduction upon arriving at base camp, we were to pick up our condoms at the orderly room before leaving for Sin City. Only, I'd never had the pleasure. According to Casey, young girls wore short, tight skirts and flashy colored blouses, and "Rock and Roll" played loudly on the jukeboxes.

Here there were no high heels, no flashy colors, just long, straight black hair and modest colors like Asian lime green, red, and black containing their thin, firm bodies.

With Ryan out of action, the young lady turned to me. "Hey, GI, I show you good time," she said, grabbing my hand and leading me into the living area; the rest followed. A bed lay behind curtains made of silk. Making myself comfortable, I followed the young lady.

Sitting on the bed, she grabbed my thigh. "I boom-boom you big-time you pay me more." It seemed like a good idea, so I gave her two more MPCs. She turned her back to me and pulled down her black silk pants, exposing a nice, round butt, then unbuttoned her blouse, dropping it to the floor, turned, and lay back against a stack of pillows at the head of the bed, exposing her womanhood. My anticipation was overwhelming. Unable to control myself, junior let me down as he erupted like Mount Vesuvius. What I had hoped would be a marathon ended in the shortest sprint to satisfaction in history. It happened so fast that the young girl got the giggles and popped up laughing. Slipping her clothes on and still laughing, she pulled the silk curtain back to rat me out. "He too fast," she blurted out. By the time I got my clothes on, I was almost too embarrassed to join the assholes.

"She boom-boom you big-time, huh," Casey said.

I paused in thought, then I responded, "Fuck you."

"Pecker problems, huh?" Freddie asked with a grin.

"Did you get your money's worth there, Jim Bob?" Casey said sarcastically.

With the laughter dying down, smiles plastered on everyone's faces except for the premature ejaculator, feeling a bit embarrassed, I said, "At least my nut sack's empty, motherfuckers."

The rest of them, passing up the opportunity to relieve themselves, exited the premises.

Walking down the dusty road leading back to the perimeter felt strange somehow. It had been months since we'd seen a city of any size.

It was getting dark now and we had to beat the curfew of seventeen hundred hours; it was back to business as usual.

An hour passed, and Charles and Greeley showed up. It was past curfew.

"The fucking MPs tried to run us out of the place at five," Charles started in. "Motherfuckers. Greeley ran their asses out."

They were in a bar close to downtown.

"How'd that happen?" I inquired.

"Wasn't no big deal, Greeley just sort of slowly moved the M16 resting on his lap, pointed it in the direction of the dickheads, slid his index finger onto the trigger, and then moved the selector switch with his thumb to full auto."

"Bet that shut 'em up?" I commented.

"You bet your sweet ass it did. The dickheads didn't say a word, didn't say goodbye, just sort of disappeared."

I grabbed my spoon and ladled a few kernels of corn from my mess kit. With the heat and humidity, the setting sun, and the noise and smells from the city drifting through the perimeter, Iowa cornfields and grandpa's farm filled my mind. I could see the hot butter melting on yellow corn, the steam disappearing high into the air, but the taste was gone.

16

Policing the Locals

Back in the Bong Son area, while we were resting and regrouping at LZ English after our ordeal in Dak To, a request for support came from Bravo Company, who were involved in a firefight in a village north of us. Orders soon followed for our company to send out two platoons and some MPs to block any locals from getting involved in the fight. Our assignment: herd up and stop the flow of any traffic from joining the battle. As we flew in, I could see old men, women, and kids moving along a road. I doubted they'd be joining any fights, but who knew the evil lurking in the minds of these country folk.

From the air, you could also see a river circling the village to the west. It looked peaceable enough, but, there again, things aren't always as they seem. We landed just south of the hamlet next to the road and moved up to block it. As a few travelers reached our roadblock, they looked bewildered and confused why they couldn't continue. As more and more reached our blockage, you could tell they were getting more agitated and pissed off at our interference. An old man started complaining loudly, which caused one of my guys to pull out his bowie knife and poke his belly like he was going to gut him or something. The old man with long whiskers, holding on to the handlebars of his bicycle, quieted down but didn't flinch, just stood there defiantly. My guy reached out with his left hand and grabbed the beard's base and sliced off half his beard with the blade, then laughed. It seemed a little excessive, but it shut him up. So much for our pacification program.

So, this military policeman said to me, "I'm out of water. Why don't you go with me, and we'll fill up our canteens from that river we saw when flying in." I was thinking, this is one stupid son of a bitch, flies out here without a full canteen. I guess he didn't grow up being a Boy Scout. Either that, or he never learned the motto, "Be Prepared!" Slipping off a few hundred yards by ourselves seemed like a terrible idea, especially knowing the enemy was in the neighborhood. But, for some dumb-ass reason, I consented.

I told him, "Yeah, sure, you want to go, then you lead the way." As we moved out, he was bebopping along like it's a Sunday walk in the park. I was thinking, you don't want to be the point man in a two-man patrol. We could still hear the sound of rifle fire off in the distance, but that didn't seem to bother him. So, he was diddy-bopping along, passing through some small empty houses, when I spotted a gook body lying against a ravine to our north. Dead as a doornail. The way he lay there with his arms laid out at weird angles, it reminded me of those Egyptian figures with the head turned sideways, his arms arranged with one arm up and broken and the other low.

So, I yelled to him, "Check out that gook to your left." At which point, the nitwit turned to me, not saying a word, his eyes the size of saucers, as if to say, "What the fuck," then lowered his head and picked up the pace to the river. I don't believe he'd ever seen a body before.

We got the water and hightailed it back to the others. An hour or two went by, the shooting north of the village died down, and Bravo Company radioed that they were calling the helicopters to exit the area. All of us were headed back to LZ English for a night of drinking beer, relaxation, and guard duty.

I thought about the MP. I imagined him playing the big man in the relative safety of the massive complex back at English. But, just hours ago, he'd found himself isolated, out of sight of the others, and came to the realization that when riding your bike without the training wheels for the first time, without the superiority of numbers in your favor, you could easily crash and burn over the need for a bit of water.

17

Screaming Eagles

She positioned her index finger just so, then, with her fingernail, picked a meaty white morsel off the scalp of the bare-breasted woman resting on her haunches in front of her. Lice: like a piece of candy, she popped it into her mouth. Then, using both hands, she went back to spreading strands of hair in search of more treats. There was something primal about the activity, something timeless about the Montagnard people.

"Where are we? Anyone know?" I asked, casting about for an answer.

"Who the fuck knows," Mason chimed in. "Somewhere north of Bong Son. That's all I know."

I liked Mason; he was one of those Neanderthal types, muscular, with lots of coarse hair, from the Central Valley. Stockton, California, is what he said.

"What do you do for a good time there in Stockton?" I asked him while leaning back against a tree and watching the lice pickers and eaters.

"Same as you. Drive up and down the main drag looking for babes." After a brief pause, he added, "We'd drive from the Dairy Queen up to the Denny's, circle around in the parking lot, then back to the DQ."

"Ever pick up any of those babes?" I asked.

"Fuck you, asshole. Of course we did."

"Oh yeah, what'd you drive? What kind of babe magnet, a Plymouth, what?"

"No, man, you can't pick up shit in a Plymouth, a '48 Merc, man."

"No shit, really?"

"Yeah."

"Chopped, lowered all the way around, painted black with white tuck and roll," he said, glancing my way, then added, "Bored-out flat head with Edelbrock dual carbs."

"Cool," I responded.

"In Berdoo, it was E Street. You know, where the McDonald brothers opened their first restaurant. The McDonald brothers live up on Little Mountain," I added. My mind wandered. The conversation bored me, so I pulled a book out of my pack and started reading. Who gives a shit about McDonald's anyhow?

"Saddle up," I heard someone bark.

I put away my book and slung the pack onto my shoulders. We were moving out, leaving the small band of natives—except for two men who agreed to scout for us.

I wondered again about our whereabouts for some reason. At least these scouts knew where the hell we were.

The hours passed, working in the same general area as the 101st—they called it a joint exercise. It wound up being an uneventful day, no enemy contact, just plodding along, occasionally smoking a Marlboro and hoping for a rest spot to escape into my book. That night, lying on my air mattress, when I closed my eyes, I thought back to the conversation with Mason. E Street, the meat burritos I bought at the Tastee Freez, the hot sauce, the case of brandy that Mike—my best friend in high school—and I stole out of the delivery truck while the driver was distracted at the ordering window, the fights we had with the boys from Rialto. Eddie, Harley, Armando, the Undertaker gang, the Rialto boys. I knew them all, mixing it up at parties and after football games—wonderful memories, hometown memories, something to squeeze out the bad shit surrounding us here.

Here we were with these little fuckers, black-pajama dudes, natives, speaking gibberish, carrying little bows with foot-long arrows, scouting, leading the way. They knew everything about the area.

Morning broke and orders came down. We were to evacuate the native people in the area—where, I didn't know. The farther we snaked through the jungle, the more mountain folk we collected, until we reached the top of a small barren hilltop with thirty or so in tow.

I'm guessing they were running from Charlie, or maybe not. Who the fuck knows. One thing was for sure, they ate the shit out of them C rations. When the choppers finally showed up, all of them were smiling, helping each other climb onto the floor of the helicopter. The two small men, our scouts, armed with bows and arrows, led us off the mountaintop and back into the dense vegetation.

Like Moses, we were lost in the wilderness—two weeks, no action. We were walking around in circles like in one of those Roy Rogers Westerns, where the good guys wear white cowboy hats while riding palominos, chasing the bad guys dressed in black, in black cowboy hats, riding black horses. As a kid, I loved watching them chase each other around the same fucking Joshua tree, the same fucking rock formation over and over, and shooting a hundred rounds out of a six-shooter, never having to reload and killing no one. Wonderful fiction. It was the same kind of fantasy we had here, only the bad guys always got away. The story never resolved; we just circled around up and down the same fucking rabbit holes.

Early morning, the light shining through the triple canopy, Casey, the last man on radio watch, looked around and noticed the little bastards were gone. No one saw them leave. They simply disappeared.

"Did anyone see the scouts leave?" the captain asked.

"No, sir, they vanished like a fart in the wind," Casey said under his breath.

"No one saw them leave," the captain said, raising his voice.

Everyone in earshot shook their heads.

Another wasted exercise. About the only good we did was feed the mountain folk.

We were meeting up with the 101st Airborne, a.k.a. Screaming Eagles, in an open area devoid of trees, just grass, but none of that fucking elephant grass that can cut you to pieces. Just meadow, a place six choppers could settle down long enough to pick us up.

A tall paratrooper approached me, his helmet held under his arm, blond hair waving in the breeze. The hotshot sergeant asked me if we'd had any luck killin' gooks.

"Nope, didn't see a fucking one. How about you?"

"Same, same, fucking waste of time." Then, surveying the area, making eye contact, he added, "Where do you guys head from here?"

"LZ English, I think," I said.

"I guess we'll find out whenever we get there," he said.

"Yup," I said.

"I got a story for you. I got this letter from a peacenik in Minnesota a while back about how we were baby killers and shit like that. So, about three weeks ago, ole Charlie ambushed us, lots of bullets spent, but we got the upper hand and blew their shit away. We didn't lose a single guy. Looking at them gook bodies, it started me to thinking about that peacenik, about how pissed off it made me. Then I got the bright idea of scooping the eyeballs out of those fucking gook heads and filling an olive jar I just happened to have with eyeballs looking every direction out of the glass cylinder. Then, the first chance I got, I mailed it to the son of a bitch." His face excited and sinister, he started laughing. "Sure would like to have been there when that bastard opened that package."

Why did he tell me that story? Was it true? Maybe. Did it matter?

I thought back to the little people picking the lice off each other's scalps, then wondered what the peacenik thought of the jar of eye candy. Maybe, "Here's looking at you, kid." The thought made me smile a bit as the sound of chopper blades rattled in the distance.

18

Candyland

"What do ya got there, man?" I asked Freddie.

"Remember, a couple of hours ago, when Eric and Frankie shot them gooks on the perimeter? Well, one of them had some weed in his knapsack."

"Yeah."

"Yeah, lucky for us, huh," Freddie said.

So Ryan, Freddie, and I made our way up to a large boulder at the center of the perimeter. In the twilight hour, Freddie handed Ryan the bag of weed Eric so graciously gave us.

Ryan expertly rolled our first doobie, licked the paper's edge, shaped it just so, and lit it up with the flick of his Zippo lighter. With it being dark now, he cupped his hand to hide the glow, took a long drag, holding his breath, then passed it to me; I did the same, keeping the smoke in as long as I could, then passing it to Freddie. It went that way for another thirty minutes—maybe an hour. Who the fuck knows. It was dark, and the big boulder was about as far away as you could get from everyone.

"Damn, that's some good shit," Freddie said.

"Damn good shit, indeed," Ryan chimed in.

"Indeed!" That was a funny word. "That's how you talk up there in Yankee land?"

Before Ryan answered, I started laughing, losing my balance, and landed on the ground. Still laughing and jolted back to some semblance of normalcy, I looked around, hoping no one noticed.

I figured we were pushing our luck, and maybe it was time to call it a night. Leastwise as far as the pot-smoking went. Knowing when to quit is a virtue, right?

I floated back to the CP for the twenty-two hundred hour shift; it was my turn to man the radios. I took control, and Casey shuffled off to catch some shut-eye. A tarp covered the table, the radios were lined up, and the handsets were lying in front of me. The light from the full moon made everything visible.

A few hours before, when the choppers had brought out the mermite cans of food, mail, and beer, they also brought sundries. Yup, it was radio watch with a buzz and time to move on to the sundries. It was all good. A box full of Baby Ruths, Jujubes, Milky Ways . . . damn, I had the munchies! Peeling back the wrapper of a Mars bar, I stuck the greatest candy bar ever made in the US of A in my mouth. The pleasure sensors went into overdrive.

"Texas League six India, over."

"Roger, this is Texas League six India, over," I responded.

"This is Texas League ten. I need to talk to your six, over."

"Roger, wait one, over."

I took another bite of the Mars bar, still marveling over the taste and thinking I'd better get a hold of six, the captain. Wait a minute, did he say the captain? Ah, shit, who the fuck did he want? And who the hell was asking?

Geez . . . there was a Baby Ruth. As I took a bite, peanut crunch and chocolate, I proclaimed out loud, "This is the greatest fucking candy bar ever!" Hell, I didn't remember liking them all that much.

Something was niggling at me. I was wondering what it could possibly be when the handset exploded.

"Where the fuck is your six, god damn it, over!" demanded the caller. *"And who am I talking to?"*

Oh, now I remembered, the fucking colonel wanted my captain.

Making my way to the captain's hooch as best I could, I announced, "The colonel wants you on the horn."

The captain finally got off the horn, then got on to me like stink on shit.

"I don't know what your fucking problem is, Soldier, but you better get your shit together, or I'll have your ass nailed to the nearest tree. You hear me?"

Fucking asshole captain killed my buzz.

Something was always dying around here.

19

Bored

Looking down, one foot in front of the other, sweaty, bored, baking in the midmorning heat, I was hoping for a little shade. The round foothills meeting the sparsely populated green valley ahead were devoid of trees. In fact, you couldn't see anything, not even a local native with one of those triangle hats working in the fields. I caught the sight of water buffalo appearing to my left, just north of us. Must have been thirty or forty of them stupid animals. Big fuckers.

Damn, it was hot. The buffalo stood maybe a hundred meters away, drinking from a wide, shallow stream—the water weaving in and around clumps of grasslike knuckles and veins like an old man's hands. By the time the stream worked its way down the canyon from behind the buffalo to us, it barely covered my boots. Wide and shallow.

Captain sensed we were all just mucking about and in need of an attitude adjustment, unlucky in our pursuit of the enemy; we lacked enthusiasm. That was our job: locate the enemy and destroy them. Only today we hadn't found any and hadn't destroyed a thing.

"Call the platoon leaders and have everyone line up on this rise facing the buffalo," the captain ordered, then added, "It'll be like shootin' ducks in a barrel."

"Yes, sir!" I answered.

"We may not have found any Cong, but we can damn sure kill their food supply," he said out loud.

Everyone followed the captain's orders, with most guys lying in the prone position, like the green army men we used to play with as kids. I always liked the prone position figure myself. He never fell over, not like the one standing up with a rifle or the bazooka guy on one knee—although, bazooka guy was pretty cool.

"Open fire!"

It sounded like one of those mad minutes we'd occasionally do first thing in the morning with everyone testing their rifles and scaring the shit out of anyone trying to sneak up on us. Only this time, rather than shooting out 360 degrees from our perimeter, we focused on the buffalo. Slowly they started to fall, knees buckling, in almost a prayerful pose—flinching, front legs first, dying one by one and eventually ending up on their sides, movement ceasing. After about thirty minutes, the only thing moving was the blood leaking from the holes in their bodies. As we righted ourselves, falling in line, moving through the shallow stream, I could see strands of thick, dark red blood reaching my boots.

I wasn't quite sure what to think about that; it seemed like such a waste. We'd began moving out to the northeast. Whether or not it helped with the boredom or our attitude, I couldn't say.

A klick and a half later, almost to the shade of the tree-filled hills, I heard an explosion. We'd passed a human hand and arm sticking up out of the dirt. The hand couldn't have been more than a week old, judging from the deterioration. Some newbie, an FNG, couldn't resist the urge to mess with it. Anybody in their right mind would have had better sense and left it alone. It was a booby trap, for sure. Never get too close to an FNG, 'cause you never know how long they'll be around.

Now, waiting for a fucking helicopter to fly in and pick up the son of a bitch, we all had to wait out in the heat just a hundred meters from the shade. I could almost hear a call from the shadows ahead, enticing us, teasing us to enter, as we sat on our steel pots and drank from our canteens. I looked down at my hand, the cigarette half-gone, then thought, *Karma's a bitch.*

20

Mad Minute

The morning was cool, and the sun was unobstructed in a cloudless sky, promising a hot day ahead.

We were moving along the bank of the creek when a chopper came out with supplies. They also brought a kid who had just been released from one of our hospitals in Japan. From what I understood, he had taken a bullet to the head a couple of months earlier. Let me restate that. His helmet took the shot while it sat on his head. But the bullet went in the front of the helmet and circled around between the steel pot and the helmet liner, then out the back—he still had the helmet. According to the docs, it scrambled the kid's brain enough; they sent him off to Japan for repair. When he was all patched up, the army figured he was ready to fight another day, as they say. Even though no physical scarring was detectable, I could tell he was agitated and scared—beyond what the rest of us felt, except for Sergeant Morgan, our communications chief, who was also overly fearful.

As we started moving again, this kid fell in behind me. Morgan was two or three soldiers ahead of me.

I turned my head and asked, "What's your name?"

"Mike."

"Are you all right?"

"Yeah, I guess," he responded.

I couldn't remember when he was hit or remember meeting him. But I started thinking about having to come back to the field after being wounded and having to face the enemy again, especially with a scrambled brain.

Walking along, I noticed some movement to the right. It was a snake entering the creek. A big fucking snake, moving at a fast rate of speed right at me. As it approached, it stopped between Mike and me and raised up as if to strike. A fucking king cobra, its head flared, standing maybe three feet high—a perfect height to strike me in the crotch. It happened so fast; I was having trouble processing the event. I froze. Then, just as fast, it lowered its body and slithered away between us and vanished into the brush.

With my breathing restored, I asked, "Hey, Mike, would you rather be taken out by a bullet or a snake?"

"Neither!"

"Good answer."

Fucking place could bite you in the ass a million ways. It started me thinking about the eight-inch-long centipede hanging above my head from a stick holding up my mosquito net. I'd thought I was being smart and decided to sleep between two logs, thus avoiding digging a foxhole. When I awoke that morning and focused my eyes, there was something moving a few inches above my nose. I realized it was one of those damn centipedes. Sliding out from underneath the mosquito net, I decided the price of my laziness was too high.

Then the image of leeches swimming alongside my air mattress popped into my head. We'd set up a perimeter in a dry rice paddy late one afternoon, popped a couple of smoke grenades so the evening chow and mail chopper could spot us, then settled in for a night's sleep. Only, no one bothered with checking the weather forecast. It rained cats and dogs, and the rice paddy filled up, unleashing the bloodsuckers. It was a long, wet night, and the last time we did a dumbass thing like that.

As the day wore on, the heat rising, stepping one foot in front of the other, I turned to take a look at Mike. His fearful eyes stared back at me. I said nothing. A moment later, a sniper fired off a burst from a brushy area to our north. We all hit the ground first then calculated our next move. Morgan and Mike looked more confused than the rest of us. The captain started shouting orders, radioing the lead platoon for assessment, and moving the company closer to the threat. Morgan and Mike were immobilized. They weren't moving. They just lay there next to the creek, hugging the ground. As we progressed, they reluctantly started moving.

I didn't hear any return fire or any additional incoming. It was just some asshole—just your average everyday sniper fucking with us.

So, we were out in Bum fuck, Egypt, and the hour was getting late. We reached a wooded area and started our routine, blowing up air mattresses, setting out claymore mines, digging foxholes—the usual stuff.

Sometime during the night, Morgan had to take a shit. Unlike the rest of us who shat outside the perimeter, he took a shit inside for fear someone on the line might forget he was out there and mistake him for the enemy. He probably would have gotten away with it, only we decided to have a Mad Minute that morning, and no one bothered with waking up the captain. Mad Minutes are when we all line up on the perimeter and fire our rifles, machine guns, grenade launchers, and the like.

Anyhow, when the shootin' started, the captain came barreling out of his hooch and stepped in Morgan's shit. Talk about one pissed-off captain.

"Who the fuck took a shit inside the perimeter?" the captain yelled as he sat down to scrape off his boot with a stick. I'm sure someone saw him do it, but no one ratted Morgan out. There wasn't much the captain could do.

"What dumb son of a bitch takes a dump in front of the captain's hooch?" I asked Ryan.

"Morgan," Ryan said.

"That figures; it was pretty damn funny, though."

"Yeah, sure was."

It turned out the captain had a few more problems than a little shit on his boot. Command pulled his ass out of the field a month later.

21

Taipei

The knock on the door startled me as I was unpacking. I went to the door, opening it a crack to see who it was. "Johnny from downstairs," answered the young lad standing outside, a fellow with a quick smile, the same fellow who had approached me downstairs in the lobby, asking if I needed a girl. He seemed a little young for that line of work, with his bangs, short-sleeve white shirt, black pants—just a tad too short—and white socks.

Opening the door farther and stepping back, I allowed Johnny to enter. "This is Joann," he announced and turned to let me get a look at the young lady he had chosen for me—a scene played out multiple times every week—week after week, an endless supply of horny GIs. The young lady, posed with one foot in front of the other, wearing a sleeveless black dress, the hemline reaching down just above the knees, was simply beautiful. Long black eyelashes, red lips, with shoulder-length black hair parted slightly to one side—fifteen bucks a day for the next five days, my escort for the week.

"Please come in," I said, thinking it was going to be a good week in this place called Taipei.

Johnny introduced us and explained the rules, the contract, the money, then left with a smile. As strangers, we moved into the room, then I sat on the desk chair. I thought her English was quite good. A fine-looking native, a well-stocked bar, safe streets, and an endless supply of Chinese food—I could get used to this. What could possibly be wrong with hanging out here for, say, the next month or two?

The Mandarin Hotel was located on a beautiful parkway filled with tall trees visible outside my second-floor room, manicured flower beds, and sculptured shrubbery. I could see the tops of taxicabs pulling in and out from under the canopy below—transportation to wherever was just a fingertip away.

"There's a bar and plenty to drink not far away," she explained.

I felt awkward in my khaki uniform but thought, what the hell. Making sure I had my key, I closed the door behind me, and we walked side by side to the elevators.

The doors slid open to a spacious lobby with a hanging chandelier; a doorman waited with his hand resting on a large vertical wooden handle.

As we approached, he asked, "May I get you a cab, sir?"

"Yes, please."

Outside, he raised his hand, signaling for a cab.

She was right; it was a short ride to the bar.

I grabbed the handle of the bar door and held it open so Joann could enter the establishment. It took a second for my eyes to adjust to the dim lights; bar girls milled about in colorful outfits, a few GIs in khakis. A GI-friendly establishment. The madam, wearing a sleeveless powder-blue silk dress with a small collar wrapped about her neck, just so, approached us from the back of the bar. With a big smile, she said, "Welcome to the Camel Bar," as she introduced herself, but I didn't catch her name. I liked her smile.

"Make yourself at home. You need anything, you come see me. OK?"

"Yes, ma'am."

Evidently, Joann, and the others, worked out of the Camel Bar. The madam slipped me several business cards with the name and address: Camel Bar, No. 25 Min Chuan Rd., E. Taipei.

The bar's mood was jovial, with plenty of laughter and made-up girls. Sitting down at one of the few empty wooden tables, I started to relax a bit. I ordered drinks—a beer for me, and whatever Joann ordered. It didn't matter. Everyone was behaving themselves, playing "Rock and Roll" and a song I didn't recognize on the jukebox.

"I like this place," I said. However, I didn't see a menu except for the drink listed above the bar.

"Good, I'm glad you like it. Where are you from in America?"

"San Bernardino. Some people call it Berdoo," I said. I didn't figure she would recognize Rialto—a bedroom community ten miles away. Then I added, "The Rolling Stones actually called it that in one of their songs, 'San Bernardino Berdoo.' It was the first time they appeared in the States." I didn't figure she knew anything about the Rolling Stones or Berdoo, but I felt the need to add it to the conversation for some odd reason.

"Sure wish I didn't have to wear this damn uniform. You know, it'd be nice to wear some civilian clothes. Walking around in this uniform, I just don't like being so obvious. I mean, well, you know."

An hour passed, and the madam sat down and asked,

"Where you grow up? What do you think of Taiwan?"

"Oh, it's great. It's a helluva lot better than where I just came from. I can tell you that much," I replied. Then I added, "California."

I took a liking to her, and Johnny the pimp. I knew it was all about the money, and if it was, so be it.

"You need civilian clothes, yes?" the madam asked. Evidently, when Joann went for a potty break, she'd mentioned it to her.

"Yeah, sure. That would be great. But where would I get some?"

"No, no, you come my house. I have clothes."

Outside, dark now with the streetlamps turned on, we grabbed a cab to the madam's house. As we drove, passing mysterious alleys here and there, shadows and foreign objects at every corner—some breathing, some not—it felt like I'd dropped into a rabbit hole like in *Alice in Wonderland*. Twenty-four hours ago, I was drinking Korean beer at the club in Cam Ranh Bay, but now the headlights were illuminating the unknown. Accompanied by Joann and the madam—the taxi driver speaking gibberish—I thought it felt strange and exciting. However, my trust was nearing the edge when we finally pulled up in front of what I hoped was the madam's apartment.

It was a small apartment, but comfy. I noticed a print on the wall, nicely framed, of Chiang Kai-shek. Another reminder of where I was. The madam offered us a seat on a small couch then went down the hall to a closet. I couldn't see what she was doing, but I figured she was thumbing through men's clothing. Finally, she pulled out a pair of dark green slacks and a short-sleeve white shirt with thin blue stripes running vertically and horizontally.

"I think these will fit you. Go ahead and try on. You can use my bedroom," she said.

"Thanks!" I said as I made my way down the hall.

"They fit perfectly," I said, from the bedroom, buttoning up the shirt, folding up my uniform.

"I thought they would. I'm pretty good at sizing up people."

I figured she'd better be, in her business. "Thank you so much. I owe you."

Back at the bar, hunger pains and too much beer started me thinking about eating something. I figured the safest food was back at the hotel. We flagged a cab, and Joann instructed the driver where to go. I grabbed the paper bag with my folded-up khakis and climbed in the back seat.

Morning arrived after a feisty night in the sack; it was time for a hot breakfast with pancakes, juice, real eggs, and coffee. Joann slipped

away for a few hours to change clothes and do whatever. I didn't ask.
"Is there anything special you want to do?" she asked in the lobby of the hotel.

"Oh, I don't know. What is there to do?" I asked.

"How about bowling? Lots of GIs like to do that," she said.

What the hell. "Yeah, let's do it."

The cab pulled up, and we hopped in. It felt like we were going south from the hotel, but it was hard to figure with the roads running in every direction but straight. The bowling alley was sitting in a parklike setting with a pagoda up against the hills. The green lawn was manicured like a golf course but greener somehow, a gardener sitting on his haunches, hand-tilling the ground surrounding a tree. The clouds were enhancing the hues; the gold-leaf two-tiered roof of the pagoda was terrific. It was held up by eight red pillars, unbelievable.

Approaching the entertainment center, I grabbed the front door handle and swung it open; sounds of pins smashing into each other reverberated off the walls. A sandwich sign at the entrance read: welcome heroes of vietnam, letters in purple surrounded by a green outline on a pink background. Weird—six months in a war zone, and you're a fucking hero. Fuck, I was done. I'd just stay here from now on, with my lady friend, and walk around dressed up in my hero outfit. Yup, that was the ticket. No use going back just to get fucked up by some gook named Charlie.

The menu—in English—listed your typical American fare. "I'll have a cup of coffee, please," I asked the waitress.

The waitress placed a fountain Coke-style glass in front of me, filled with coffee with floating ice cubes. What the fuck was that, ice in the coffee? Whoever heard of such a thing? Taking a sip—trying to keep an open mind—I decided it tasted pretty damn good. Who knew?

"No bowling for me. Do you want to bowl?" I asked Joann.

"No, no!"

Apparently, certain places catered to GIs and escorts. I finished my coffee and checked my watch, wondering if it was too early to start drinking.

"You want to go somewhere else?" she asked.

"Yeah, let's go back to the Camel Bar."

Back at the bar, we were surrounded by five or six unencumbered escorts, ordering drinks, making small talk, when one of them mustered up the courage to ask me if I'd read a letter for her. "Yeah, sure." With a big smile, she fished around in her purse and pulled out a letter, the return address reading 25th infantry apo in San Francisco.

"What it say?" she asked impatiently.

"Dear Barbara, I've missed you so much . . ." I continued reading as she listened intently. I'm sure she was trying to remember every word. Perhaps she could get someone to write a letter in English for her—write it to her special John. As I read the letter, the other girls started digging in their purses. When I lifted my head and looked around, a dozen escorts held up letters for me to read. I felt like I couldn't turn them down. I grabbed the closest letter, and being the kind gentleman that I am, I obliged. Most of them were a bit sappy, but then, it was a bit of humanity written in the sweltering heat, maybe a barracks, maybe sitting on a helmet in the jungle somewhere. Letters scribbled on paper with ink pens and pencils, letters filled with a hope of extending those memories, a future, possibilities outside the Nam, feeling valued somehow, that their union meant more than a little money.

"I'm hoping the army will let me take leave so I can see you again," a lonely GI wrote. It was a lie; the army didn't grant leaves from the Nam. He was hoping against hope that somehow the angels would reach down and make it so, like the fairy tales told to children.

For dutifully reading the letters, I became somewhat of a celebrity. The madam asked if I would do her a favor. "There's navy base not far from here; if I got you a cab and gave you money, would you buy some Maker's Mark whiskey for me?"

"Yeah, sure." What the hell. A mile or two away, I showed my military ID at the PX/BX—I never knew the difference—and I grabbed three bottles of whiskey. The distinctive red rubberlike seal dripped down the side of the cap onto the bottle. I started thinking on the way back, with Joann by my side: maybe I could earn my keep and stay awhile buying cheap liquor for the bar. Who knew, maybe there'd be other shady things I could do.

"You number one. Thank you, thank you," the madam said with a big smile.

Nighttime was fast approaching, and Joann asked if I wanted to go to the movies. It sounded like a good idea to me. "Hell yes, let's go." A fancy place by anyone's standards, the theater was beautiful, a stage that could be elevated for concerts or lowered, allowing movies to be shown.

It reminded me of the California Theatre on 4th Street in San Bernardino, only better. The main feature starred Paul Newman in the movie *Hombre*—Mr. Blue Eyes raised by Indians dressed up like a cowboy acting the compassionate badass. It seemed a bit funny looking around at the audience reading Chinese subtitles. Then again, I felt a little weird too when I realized I was the only round-eye in the place, wearing a white shirt with thin blue stripes in a checkered pattern. All the men wore plain white shirts and dark pants.

Everyone seemed to enjoy the movie, though, a real shoot-'em-up with the evil Richard Boone making life hell for everyone. The western landscape reminded me of the days I'd spent in Southern California's high desert mountains trying to shoot jackrabbits with an iron-sight .22. It dawned on me: the jackrabbits were a lot like Charlie. You'd see them two hills away, too far for a good shot. So you'd go down one hill and up the next. Then, off in the distance, the fucking rabbit was still two hills away. You could never get close enough for a decent shot. Jackrabbits are evil that way. Either that or, like Charlie, they're smarter.

The next morning, Joann and I decided to visit the Yangmingshan National Park just north of the city. Sitting in a boat with twenty passengers or so, we crossed a wide, shallow river—shallow enough that a thin young man with a long pole buried in the water, pushing against the bottom, could move us to the mountainous park. A canyon leads up to a waterfall, the main event—nothing like Niagara Falls, mind you, just a small stream of water cascading down the rocks against the steep mountain walls. Shops lined the small pedestrian road, and we passed the occasional rickshaw, big enough to carry two people.

It was another beautiful day, Joann dressed in white, with beige-colored shoes and long eyelashes caked with mascara.

The last night back at the hotel, Gary, a fellow from the 2nd platoon, knocked on my door.

"What's up, man?" I asked as I opened the door.

"Hey, can you help me out? I mean, can you help out Walter? He spent all his money, man." Walter was a black kid I didn't know well from South Carolina. Why didn't he come to me directly? Weird. Gary, from South Carolina, said Walter felt more comfortable asking him. I figured it for a Southern thing.

"Yeah, I can help." As I pulled my wallet out of my back pocket, I said, "I can spare a twenty. Will that do?"

"That'll work. Thanks, man."

The lights started illuminating in the street outside, the hour getting late. It was my last night, Joann already in bed. I started writing at the desk against the wall opposite the bed. Twenty, maybe thirty minutes went by, and Joann asked if I was coming to bed.

"No, I'm going to write for a while; besides, I figured you could use a break for the evening."

That was not what she had in mind, because passion filled the room, unlike any other night. When morning broke, I could hear her showering as I packed my stuff, leaving out the clothes the madam had loaned me. As I checked out, folding up the rice-paper receipt at the hotel desk, she asked, "Maybe you can stay; I have a place you could stay. It's on the coast." I didn't answer right away. What if I did stay? What would happen? I'd get caught for sure. Was it worth six months in the Saigon prison, or was it better to go back and get my ass shot off?

The army bus showed up on the parkway. GIs milling about in the foyer started filing out.

"I'll write." Those were my last words to Joann. Then, turning, I grabbed the rail handle and climbed the stairs.

22

Welcome to the I Corps

"This sure beats the shit out of humping," I said to Casey.

"No shit," he said with a smile, curly hair blowing in the breeze, the steel pot helmet resting against his leg.

Mason was digging away in the pit of our would-be bunker with his shirt off, filling his shovel with scoop after scoop of dirt, then letting it fly high out of the hole.

"Did your mother ever tell you you're a pussy?" yelled Freddie.

"Fuck you!" answered Mason as another scoop of dirt flew into the air.

"I bet your old lady's banging Jody right about now," Freddie continued.

Mason didn't say a word and kept digging. Only room for one poor bastard in the hole at a time.

"You get that Dear John letter yet?" Casey chimed in.

It was midday, hotter than hell; I took a swig of my cherry-flavored Kool-Aid. The captain and the first sergeant, sitting on sandbags, were shooting the breeze when an order came down from Battalion.

Out of the blue, the captain announced, "Get your shit together; we're moving out."

"Now what?" I asked Casey.

Mason unscrewed the nut on the entrenching tool, folding the blade flat against the handle, climbed out of the would-be bunker, and said, "Who knows?"

"What's going on?" Freddie asked.

"I don't know, man, but the choppers are on their way," I answered.

We were helicoptered back to An Khê, where two C-130s were ready on the tarmac; we hustled aboard. Leaning back against the fuselage, I asked Freddie, "Where you think we're headed this time?"

"I don't know, man. Your guess is as good as mine."

"Usually, they tell us where we're headed," I said.

"Not this time," Freddie said.

When we left An Khê and headed north, word started circulating we were on our way to the I Corps. The speed at which the powers that be told us to load up our shit and move out caused considerable anxiety, like the time we flew out to Dak To. But this time, it felt more ominous. At least they'd told us where we were headed that time.

We landed in Chi Lai; the base was huge, C-130s flying in and out, fighter jets, spotter planes, navy radar planes, you name it. As we made our way from the planes to the choppers, there was a utility truck just to our left with two large stainless steel milk containers with white tubes crimped to hold in the contents—one container with whole milk and the other with chocolate milk. Of my eight months in the field, this was the first time I'd tasted real milk. I was used to canned milk, but fresh milk? What a treat . . . or so I thought. I downed several canteen cups full of both. Damn, it was so good. But as we lifted off for our final destination, my stomach started to churn and ache. With my body in full revolt, we arrived at LZ Ross.

With the rain coming down in buckets—fucking monsoons—LZ Ross looked chaotic. The Marines were readying themselves to move north toward the DMZ.

On first impression, the thing about the Marines that interested me most was they still carried the M14. Impressive, really. It fired a decent bullet, not like the wimpy .223. The only issue I could see was the weight and length of the rifle and the limited amount of ammo you could carry.

This being the I Corps, the captain ordered us to wear two bandoleers holding six mags each, crisscrossing our chests like Pancho Villa. With six more mags in each one of my ammo pouches, that made twenty-four. Then, of course, one in the rifle made for a total of twenty-five. Each mag had 19 rounds, totaling 475 rounds per grunt. That's a lot of goddamn firepower provided the piece-of-shit rifle doesn't jam. You had to be careful not to add that extra round, based on my experience.

"Well, I tell you, it ain't been a cakewalk around here," I heard the navy doctor tell the captain. "We lost a lot of guys."

"Where you headed?" the captain asked.

"North, that's all I know."

I turned to Ryan. "What do you think, man?"

With the rain still pounding the green canvas tent, he added, "We're pretty much fucked."

The next day, the sun burning through the clouds and finally chasing the rain away, a big fucking crane helicopter showed up, squatting like a spider over the big guns, attaching long straps, one by one, lifting 105s, stacks of ammo on pallets, artillery rounds, communication supplies, all the things you need to sustain a battalion in the field. After a couple of days, all the equipment had been moved, along with the Marines, to where: who knew.

Freddie sat at the mouth of my hooch, drinking one of our two beer allotments for the day. "I got a letter from your sister the other day. She seems nice. I see she's going to Mankato State in Minnesota," I said.

"Yeah, she's a good kid. I gave her your address a while back," Freddie said.

"How far is that from Fort Dodge?" I asked.

"It's a little more than a hundred miles due north."

"She warned me about your card playing."

"Yeah, I wouldn't pay her any mind," Freddie said.

Then, turning his attention to the present and the Marines, he asked, "What do you think? Where do you think them sons of bitches are going?"

"North. You know as much as I do," I said, staring out at the mountain range to the north.

"Across the DMZ?" Freddie asked.

"Maybe. I think the navy doctor thought that might be a possibility," I said.

"Jesus Christ, if them bastards cross the DMZ, we're in for the duration."

"You think?" I said, not having connected the dots.

"You can bet your sweet ass on it," Freddie replied, then continued, "If Johnson orders them, ain't nothing nobody can do." Contemplating a couple of minutes, he then added, "It ain't looking good, man."

As I finished my warm beer, I said, "You got that right."

Although I appreciated the Marines, the stories about getting their asses kicked in two major fights here set my nerves on edge. Now, it was up to us to hold this valley, to get to know this valley, to live or die in this valley. We hadn't been back to base camp going on eight months now. Fuck, we'd never been back to base camp as a unit. It wasn't like they told us eight months ago. Like we'd be in and out of

An Khê pulling easy duty every month or so. But no, no fucking Sin City, no easy perimeter watch, no decent chow, no USO shows.

As I was deep in my pity party mood, Freddie blurted out, "You know the gooks got prices on our heads."

"Yeah, how's that work?"

"Fuck if I know."

"Like in the Old West: bounties, wanted dead or alive kinda shit. How do you claim a kill, get your money, take a fucking photograph?" I asked.

"I don't know nothing about that. But, if I did, what do you figure a gook gets for killing one of us?" Freddie asked.

"I'm guessing it depends on whether or not it's an officer, a radioman, a machine gunner, or whatever."

"Do you remember how long the radioman lasts in a firefight?" Freddie asked.

"Fifteen seconds, some say less."

"Fifteen seconds. What about a chaplain?" Freddie said with a smile.

"Nothing, man, they wouldn't waste no fucking bullets on a chaplain. Besides, they're always late to the party anyhow."

"Let's hope Charlie doesn't collect no bounties today," Freddie added as he got up to walk back to his platoon.

23

Eight-ball

Flying low over the valley, over the occasional thatched roof, the rice paddies, and islands of palm trees, then jumping the short distance to the ground, I heard automatic gunfire not far away. Eight-ball cut down the son of a bitch we saw from the air. A North Vietnamese soldier dressed in his Sunday best. He was walking around like he owned the place. That is, until he heard us coming. He was caught out in the open, no place to run, no place to hide, and Eight-ball riddled his fancy uniform with bullets. He lay motionless on the dirt path.

"Sorry about the uniform, motherfucker," Eight-ball said to the limp body as he rolled him over and lifted a pistol from his holster.

"Hey, man, nice pistol," he said. Then on closer inspection, "Russian made. How about that? Now that's a respectable trophy, don't ya think?"

"Yeah, man, don't get no better than that," I said.

Rifling through his pack and pockets, Eight-ball pulled out a bundle of money and a sheet of paper with chicken scratch written on it.

"What's this fucker doing with all this money? Gotta be an important dude, maybe a paymaster or something. That's a lot of goddamn piaster."

"No shit, man, a lot of fucking moola," I said, echoing Eight-ball.

We fucked up his day and took his money and his Russian pistol. Eight-ball tagged the pistol for his own, then handed the money over to the captain, who handed it over to me.

Damn, we hadn't taken a single casualty and, as near as I could tell, we were a helluva lot richer. Leastwise until the fucking intelligence officer showed up.

Scattered out to sweep the area like a pinball machine, platoons pinging off objects, finding different lanes to go down, dikes with the sun burning bright with little wind and searing heat—it started me thinking that we'd finally surprised the bastards for a change. It was going to be a good day.

Eight-ball, from the 2nd platoon, was a hard-nosed and trusted leader. With three stripes up and one down—army-green background with black chevrons—on his arm, he could be counted on in a firefight. With sandy blond hair and a determined demeanor, he didn't hesitate to pull the trigger. I liked that about him. Along the way, he had taken a ballpoint pen and drawn a Magic 8 Ball on his camouflage helmet cover. And magic it was.

On a dike to the left of Eight-ball—maybe fifty meters or so away now—I heard automatic fire again. Eight-ball was about to step over a spider hole in the dike when he jumped back, throwing his arm out in front of him with his hand on the pistol grip, pulling the trigger. A gook waiting at the bottom of the spider hole, his AK pointed skyward, hesitated, but Eight-ball didn't. Two kills inside of two hours.

"You get the son of a bitch?" I yelled across the paddy.

"You bet your sweet ass I did," Eight-ball yelled back.

Thirty minutes passed, and in the distance we saw an elevated mount, an island of sand and dirt, an oasis several feet above the paddy; I saw the point man start climbing, careful with his footwork. As Eight-ball approached the mound, he noticed a spider hole. Only this one was dug into the bank a few meters from where the column was making its climb. And once again, he got off the first shots.

Once the dust settled, Freddie shouted, "What are you, man, a fucking gunslinger? The fastest draw in the Nam!"

But, this time, a bonus: a woman surprised us by crawling out of a hole to our right, raising her hands, and surrendering, leaving her AK behind.

"Fertile ground, don't ya think, gooks hiding every fucking where," I said to Freddie.

"No wonder the Marines got their ass kicked up here. NVA motherfuckers probably all over these fucking mountains," Freddie said.

Obviously, these mountains were riddled with underground bunkers and tunnels. The Marines would just fight it out until they took the mountaintop no matter the body count. Then it was back to base to wait on reinforcements. Like a yo-yo, they'd do it all over again. That's what the navy doctor told the captain when we first showed up at Ross. The rain was pouring down. Amid confusion in the command tent, the navy doc told Captain Hartley the Marines lost more than 300 guys in each of the two major battles they fought here. I didn't hear how many of the enemy died.

I got to thinking about the drawing on Eight-ball's helmet, about all the shit written or drawn on our camo helmet covers. Girlfriends' names from back in the world, peace symbols, or whatever blew our skirts up. Then there was Eight-ball. Was there a connection between the crude scribbling on our helmet, the brass bracelets encircling our wrists, and making it out of this hellhole? Was it the right drawing, the right name, the graphic? As for the brass band, you didn't dare take it off. Superstitious. Hell yes, I was still carrying a two-by-three-foot piece of peach-colored silk woven with an Oriental design I'd bought from a pregnant hooker in a small village outside of Bong Son. It didn't make sense, and I don't know why, it's just what you did.

It was getting late now and time to look for a place to set up a perimeter, scout the surrounding area, fire in defensive targets, and figure out where to place our radios.

Casey and Mason decided to pocket a few thousand. No one would be the wiser; we were doing the counting. I didn't think it was right for some dumbass reason. It was that karma thing, the superstition thing again. Blood money. Besides, how the hell was I going to launder the money? There were no friendlies around here catering to our every need. We weren't bloody likely to get back to base camp anytime soon. It wasn't like you could wander into headquarters and hand over a thousand dollars' worth of piaster and exchange it for MPCs.

Casey was looking for some bamboo to cut down to support the hooch, dragging poles back, laying them on the ground. I snapped together our ponchos, draped them over the cross members, and staked down the corners. Casey tied and staked the head openings, where your noggin went, to keep the ponchos from leaning in. The last thing: tie the mosquito net in place. It was our usual shit after every movement; now to dig the foxholes and schedule radio watch—midnight, two, four.

I pulled out the eight-and-a-half-by-eleven sheet of paper the USO gave me a few months back after R & R. Printed on it was a drawing of a helmet with boots below, a getting short illustration. Like a puzzle, it was broken up into a hundred pieces, representing your last hundred days in country. I pulled out my pen and filled in another piece, ninety-three days to go. Then I reflected on my first rodeo in the I Corps.

24

Ambushed Again

Sixteen hundred hours in the afternoon, it was time to set up a perimeter, dig foxholes again. We were still several klicks from base camp, and the sandy area, palm trees, and natural barriers we found ourselves in seemed a perfect location. It was time to scout the area in front of us, find a place to set up a listening post for the night. Gotta keep them evil ones from sneaking up on us.

"Everly, take your platoon and scout the area in front of us," Captain Hartley ordered.

"Yes, sir," responded Lieutenant Everly.

Lieutenant Everly was short by platoon leader standards but very capable. His men liked him. He didn't push back on the captain's order; he simply said to his men, "Saddle up."

The empty, sandy area with plenty of tree cover served as a good place to camp for the night. The field of fire was decent in all directions. At the lower level of the area was a twenty-meter span to the dike to the south, with the dry rice paddy elevated three feet or so above. Then it was another forty meters to the next elevated dike separating yet another, higher rice paddy, a mosaic of terraces. Eight-ball led the way, followed by Lieutenant Everly, then his radio operator and the rest of the platoon. Eight-ball had just reached the far side of the rice paddy, just barely to the wall of the dike. Having escaped his notice were two spider holes on either side of him, the platoon strung out single file behind him. I heard automatic fire. I was looking for some bamboo poles to make a hooch when I turned toward the sound. Everly was already down, shot to hell, lying face down, his helmet lying next to his blond hair, his hand on the grip of his rifle. I don't believe he even got a shot off. The radio operator, Bobby, was barely moving, his helmet lying off to one side, the handset still attached to his webbing. But his movements told me he was finished. Martin and Carter were closest to us but still out of reach. Bullets were penetrating their fatigues, ripping holes in their bodies, the fabric moving with each bullet, creating a mini-explosion as they lay there. All had been caught off guard; all of them lay down pumped full of lead, except for Eight-ball.

A female UPI photographer traveling with us moved up close behind the berm, close enough to focus her Nikon lens and snap photos of the motherfuckers, capturing them spraying 39mm bullets from their AKs. Unbelievable. There lay my guys and Eight-ball with his back against the wall, pinned there. They couldn't shoot him, and he couldn't shoot them. He was trapped, no-man's-land. Captain Hartley moved everyone up against the berm, the ground just high enough that if you were crouching, the bullets couldn't find their mark. The first sergeant started acting the fool, stooped over, running up and down behind the men, barking nonsense. For a base camp paper pusher to be running with one hand on his helmet, his knees almost finding his chin, it almost made me laugh. He didn't appear to know shit from Shinola when it came to a firefight. Showboating, that's all it was.

With four lying in the dry rice paddy, motionless, getting the others—the ones trying to crawl back over the berm, the wounded—out of the rice paddy was job one. Firing back, Freddie and a few others took off their packs and slipped over the berm and low-crawled up to the guys lying in pain, the ones who couldn't make it on their own. The rest of us lined up behind the berm, firing, suppressing enemy fire.

A radio transmission from Bravo Company announced they were in place to our right. I couldn't see them for all the vegetation but could hear the fire. It worried me a bit that they didn't know our location or the situation. With bullets flying from what seemed like everywhere now, nothing felt safe. With one hand grabbing under a man's arm, pulling, trying to rescue one of our own, struggling to drag him over the berm, Freddie flinched, dropped his arm, and grabbed his stomach. Gutshot. Fuck. Fetching a poncho, two of us pulled on his clothing, sliding him over the berm, and laid him on the poncho. Ryan and Mason joined us, grabbing the corners and moving bent over like the first sergeant. We were moving as fast as we could, making it up an embankment where a medevac was landing. As we maneuvered him onto the floor of the chopper, Freddie, with one hand holding his gut, looked our way and held up his thumb with the other. Then the chopper lifted off. Freddie was finally out of the shit. The son of a bitch finally made it out of the field. *The motherfucker better not die on me,* I thought.

Eight-ball was still pinned against the dike when the captain came up with the bright idea to bring another chopper in to lay down smoke. If we could lay down enough smoke, maybe Eight-ball could make it back. That was the plan. It was a bit dicey for the chopper with bullets zinging everywhere, the chopper pilot flying low, approaching from our left through no-man's-land to drop the smoke canisters. With the door gunner's machine gun laying down fire full bore against the dike and beyond, just maybe there was a chance. A helluva ballsy move, I must say—fucking chopper pilots always came through when you needed them.

With the rice paddy starting to fill with smoke, thick clouds pouring out of the canisters, the dike and Eight-ball almost disappearing, it was now or never. He started running, zigzagging back and forth, headed for us. In the wispy smoke, I could see the bullets kicking up the dirt and sand at his feet as he emerged from the cloud a half step ahead of death. Jumping over the berm, the son of a bitch made it unscathed.

That night, after everything calmed down, the wounded safely evacuated, the dead loaded up and gone, I'd just finished my turn on radio watch and lay down on my air mattress. I could hear Top and the captain still discussing the day's events and I heard the first sergeant tell the captain,

"I'll get the paperwork ready; we can recommend each other for Silver Stars."

The captain was silent, didn't say a word.

I took out the little green memo book, the one where I kept track of head counts, supplies, and who owed whom from our poker games. Eighty-five MPCs, that's what I owed Freddie. Nobody beat Freddie at cards. Maybe someday he'd come to collect. I could hope.

25

Dane

Looking east toward the empty lot across from my house, I saw Dane Lattimer ride his Schwinn bicycle with a big basket attached to the handlebar, supports bolted to the axle of the front wheel. The rumor was he was a child molester; I didn't know about that, but all of us neighborhood kids gave him a wide berth. At my young age, he looked old and peculiar. He always wore gray workman's clothes, the kind they sold at Sears, Roebuck in San Bernardino. He had a gaping mouth full of ugly teeth and breathed hard as he rode, rhythmically pedaling, favoring his right leg and using it as a power stroke, his head bobbing back and forth as he moved closer to his parents' house, a stone's throw from where I slept.

Gilbert, from the 4th platoon, whose job was to carry mortar rounds, reminded me of Dane, an outcast living at the edge of accepted society.

It was zero four hundred hours in the morning, the third night maneuver in eight months. The one back in Bong Son months ago had resulted in no kills, no captures, no nothing. The second one, we'd surrounded a village before dawn then called in Willie Pete artillery rounds, hoping to spook the little bastards, thinking they would flee the village like rats from a sinking ship. Geez, where do you suppose all those baby sons come from if their men, in their black pajamas, aren't slipping into the house at night for a little rest and recuperation and bebopping the old lady? After the twenty or so rounds landed, exploding, causing mayhem, it was time to move in. But all I saw was a bunch of women and kids scurrying about in this remote mountain village, looking for a place to hide. With gaping mouths, their cries and screams echoing in my ears. A mother running past me held a young child, maybe two or three, with white phosphorus burning its way through the kid's arm. I asked myself, *Where the hell was she going? Ain't like there's a clinic around here.* And again, no kills, no captures, no nothing, just a bunch of fucked-up civilians. Another failed mission.

Maybe our third attempt at night moves would finally result in some measure of success. But damn, it was dark—one of the darkest nights I can remember. When word passed from one to the next that we were moving out, I couldn't see shit. I had to feel around on the ground to make sure I wasn't leaving something behind. As we all struggled to get up, squaring away our ammo pouches and packs, our only option at this point was to hold on to the belt of the man in front of us and hope like hell the chain didn't break. It's not like you could start yelling for help or ordering folks around. Everyone had to speak in whispers. The whole point was to surprise the enemy, to catch them with their pants down, if you will. Then it occurred to me, who the fuck knew where the point man was taking us? He couldn't see any better than I could.

As we stumbled up and down small hills and across flat land, the sky finally started to lighten. The point man had successfully led us through the early hours of the morning, and we emerged from complete darkness without a single incident.

We'd reached a place to rest and gather ourselves at the base of a mountain.

A voice behind me shouted, "Where the hell are your mortar rounds,

Gilbert?"

Gilbert had either failed to load up the mortar rounds in the dark, or he'd figured out how to ditch them without the guy behind him knowing it. It didn't make sense. It's not like you wouldn't know. The son of a bitch probably never loaded them up in the first place.

"Where the fuck are your mortar rounds? Goddamn, man, where are they?" demanded Sergeant Miller.

Miller was one big SOB, big enough to carry around the baseplate of an 81mm mortar with ease. He wasn't one to play coy with; he was a hard-nosed son of a bitch, and Gilbert—slight in build, maybe five-seven—needed to come up with an acceptable answer. Only he couldn't.

"They must have worked their way out somehow," he pleaded.

"And you didn't notice, you dumb fuck?"

From the rage in Miller's eyes, I felt certain that if no one were around to witness, he would have killed him right then and there.

Gilbert, his eyes darting about, avoiding everyone's scorn, nervously moving about as if looking for an escape, had just given the Cong the means to booby-trap us with our own fucking munitions.

Finally, the captain shouted to saddle up and cut short the exchange. Starting up the steep grade of the mountain, searching for higher ground, exposing us to the valley below, Gilbert, now in front of me, slipped and lost his footing. With his M16 switched to full auto, a burst of rounds fired off to the right as his rifle hit the ground and he impulsively squeezed the trigger. Everyone was hugging the ground, trying to assess the danger. If Charlie was in the neighborhood, we were all fucked, exposed and open, just like that exposed paymaster Eight-ball shot up a while back.

This is where Gilbert and Dane Lattimer differ: Dane would have gotten home with the mortars. He'd have placed them in his bicycle's basket and labored with a gaping mouth, power-stroking his right leg to safely get them there.

I'd take Dane over Gilbert any day.

26

The Foot

There it was—something out of the ordinary registering in my peripheral vision. A foot hiding in a hole dug into the side of a sandy embankment. The area was shaded by palm trees and lay just to the north of a rice paddy barely filled with water. The midday sun's reflection kept pace with us as we trudged along the edge. The rice peeked out of the shallow water just like this old man's foot, not quite concealed. The twenty guys ahead of me walking single file must have been too absorbed in the far-off surroundings or consumed with the ever-present boredom, imagining a life lived previously, back in the world. Perhaps I wasn't the only one to see the foot hiding. If the guys ahead of me did see it, they evidently didn't think it was worth the trouble to investigate, or they simply wanted to get to the next resting place. Who knows why?

It appeared to be an old foot, or so it seemed, with crusty mud stuck to its heel and between its toes, attached to an ankle and a leg disappearing into the shadow. I notified the captain, and he had me radio the lead platoon to stop.

Hank yelled at the hiding shadow, *"Lai day, lai day,* motherfucker!" But there was no movement. He repeated it three more times and still no response. Then he pulled the pin on a smoke grenade and threw it into the hole. It was resting an inch or two from the crusty foot before it ignited. Red smoke started billowing out of the spider hole. The light wind dispersed the smoke, and it wisped out and away from the hole. I couldn't hear if the man was choking or not, but I figured he was holding his breath, closing his eyes, and praying to his ancestors for help until the grenade burned itself out.

I knew the locals feared us. They were told stories of how we mistreated prisoners, and there was the fear of retribution by the NVA or local Cong if they cooperated with us. But damn, you'd think he would crawl out of that hole rather than face certain death.

Hank tossed in a real grenade this time. Preparing for the blast, we scattered out on both sides of the hole. But nothing happened. A fucking dud. Sure enough, here was this gook coiled up in the fetal position with a smoke grenade and a dud nesting next to his foot, and he still refused to exit. Hank tossed in another one, another dud. What were the chances of two duds? A smoke, two defective grenades, and now what? Pulling the pin, the handle flying off, waiting a few seconds, then tossing it in. Don't give the gook time to toss it back out. But the third one meant business and ended the drama. No more gook. Chalk up another one in the book of life and death. Pencil in another kill on the scorecard.

I didn't bother to look at the result of the blast, whether it exploded the duds or not. I just sat on the ground, slid my arms through the straps of my pack, adjusted the bandoleers crisscrossing my chest, and pushed myself up.

As we continued to skirt the edge of the rice paddy, headed for LZ Ross, the what-ifs crept into my mind, but I soon moved on to dreaming about driving around in a white Chevy Impala, maybe up E Street in San Berdoo, and grabbing a burger at McDonald's. I looked down at my right hand and wondered if the ringworm growing there would ever go away.

27

Letter from Home

Using my finger, I ripped the envelope open—a letter from home, the return address written in blue ink, more often than not a typewritten letter enclosed. Both of my parents could type like crazy. My mother was a secretary for the big boss at Kaiser Steel in Fontana, and dad, an independent businessman. Images of my dad popped into my head, pounding away frantically on his manual Underwood typewriter like he was killing a demon inside, the keys smacking the paper hard enough to imprint more than one carbon copy.

As I slid the contents out of the envelope and unfolded the typewritten letter, a newspaper clipping fell to the ground: an announcement of the marriage of Helen Ann Peterson and William M. Hitchens. Why my mother thought it a good idea to include a wedding announcement from a former girlfriend was baffling. Did she not know that Helen was my first love, that we dated the last two years of high school? Now there she was, wearing a veil that her parents brought back from their recent trip to Europe, a bouquet in her hands, with William's hands covering hers. William was a tall, goofy-looking dude with wavy red hair, black-rimmed glasses, a protruding round chin, and a forehead way too big. But he had one thing—actually two things: the brains I didn't have to get into UC Berkeley and, consequently, my girl.

Reading the newspaper clipping, I noticed William didn't have a middle name, just an "M." I wondered about that. Why did they print her middle name and not his? What the fuck did it matter, anyhow? It went on . . . Reverend Willard Roberts had performed the rites. Why do they call it rites? Is it because you can't legally boink the bride without some guy in a suit or a robe, speaking holy words?

Looking a little closer, studying my former classmate, I noticed William's skinny neck was much too small for the collar surrounding it. Again, what did it matter? He won the day. I wasn't in William's league, and he knew it. What was a girl to do, make a go of it with someone with no prospects, or someone who could provide for her in a fashion she was accustomed to—the daughter of a doctor? I put the letter away, folding up the clipping and slipping it back into the envelope without finishing.

Interrupting my thoughts, bombs started dropping high from the night sky: a B-52's strike on the far side of the Que Son Valley targeting the mountain range, a thundering sound, the lights—like a Technicolor movie just a few miles away—fucking impressive like nothing I'd ever seen. Those tunnels dug into the mountain range were no match for an airstrike of this size. The pounding went up and down the mountain range, pounding, pounding, deeper and deeper—penetrating—lights pulsing again and again in the mushroom clouds of dirt and dust. Then it was over, and calm filled the air. The dust was dissipating, filtering softly through the trees like a blanket covering a freshly scarred wound.

Lying on my air mattress, I covered my head with a poncho liner, slid the metal switch up to turn on my crook-neck flashlight, and began reading the clipping again.

"They were married in the bride's residence . . . " it continued. I'd spent many a night after a date parked in that driveway in my '55 blue Chevy, kissing, hoping for something more, her father in the living room reading his medical books, keeping up with the latest discoveries, procedures, and drugs. "A candlelight ceremony . . ." it went on. How fucking romantic. "Daisies and mums, yellow and white . . . " How would he like a yellow smoke grenade stuck up his ass? I took a swig of Kool-Aid, then reading of champagne and punch further depressed me.

Why would my mother send me such a clipping? A honeymoon in San Francisco. How fucking nice for them.

I stuck the envelope and the clipping into the vinyl gas mask container where I kept all the letters I got from the world. Why save it? Who the fuck knows.

28

Casey's Peeing Adventure

Casey, my New York City boy, and I had already weathered a lot of shit together. He did more than his share of drugs growing up—so he said. He was a tall, curly-haired soldier. He had an easy smile and was quick to laugh. Everyone liked him. He did his job handling the radios, filling sandbags, digging foxholes, burning shit, whatever. He never complained . . . much. What I liked most about him was his sense of humor.

"How was R and R, man?" Mason asked.

"Beautiful, man!" Casey said with excitement. "Hong Kong is great, and the women, wow! You gotta go to Hong Kong, man. You're going next week, right?"

"Yup, that's what Top told me," Mason replied. "I'm leaving the field the day after tomorrow."

"There's this beautiful girl named Charlotte that works out of the Jasmine Bar not far from where they take all us motherfuckers," Casey said.

"Yeah, man, whatever you say. She's good, huh?"

"Hell yes, she is. Unbelievable!" Casey confirmed.

The day arrived, and Mason was on the Huey headed for base camp where he'd collect some money and pack his bag, then a brief stop in Cam Ranh Bay, where the commercial jets ferried you to Japan, Australia, Thailand, Hawaii, you name it. Mason got on the Hong Kong express. Ain't nothing like getting out of the field to someplace safe.

Meanwhile, while we were camped on top of a hill—LZ Edward, or Nui Loc Son—in the south end of the Que Son Valley, safeguarding 105mm howitzers, huddled in our bunker—thanks to the Marines who dug them—playing cards, Casey had to take a pee. Normally, that wasn't a big deal. Only this time, we could hear whimpering at the edge of the perimeter. Something was seriously wrong.

When Casey finally returned, Ryan asked him, "What the fuck's up with you? Why were you crying out there, man?"

"It hurts, man. It hurts to pee. There's something wrong with my dick."

"Yeah, something wrong with your dick; you'd better see Doc before the damn thing falls off."

After seeing Doc and hearing about the diagnosis, Casey pondered the question of how he could have possibly gotten gonorrhea.

"Where the hell could I have contracted it? There ain't no booty to be had around here," he wondered out loud. None of us responded when he finally settled on an answer: Hong Kong. That little bitch Charlotte.

Even though we all liked Casey, we were secretly enjoying the muffled cries from the edge of the perimeter. Our sick humor rose as we heard another scream coming from the edge of the danger zone. Only it wasn't long before we were all suffering from our own problems. Yup, you guessed it. We all started scratching our balls and pubic hair—Casey's payback time.

The only outhouse we'd had access to in months with a real sit-down toilet was alive with crabs. Rather than having to squat to take a dump, we were shitting like regular folks back in the world, enjoying a touch of civilization by sitting. We were clueless and unsuspecting of the little bastards finding their way to our nut sacks and crawling up to the bushy area above our schlongs. There, a different enemy set up shop, forcing us to reach down, clawing at our privates every few minutes, as the sweat added fuel to their newly found paradise. There's nothing like going on patrol, dodging bullets, reading books, playing cards, and keeping one hand in your pants, fighting the war between your legs.

Doc ordered up some sort of pasty cream to kill off the little bastards. With Casey peeing razor blades and a half dozen of us grabbing our crotches, it wasn't our finest hour.

I began to worry about Casey. Poor fucker, maybe he'd end up sterile, maybe no rug rats in his future. It seemed like it took forever to get Casey the medicine he needed.

Mason finally finished up his week of R & R and arrived with the evening helicopter, along with mermite cans full of hot chow, ammo, beer, and mail.

Lining up to go through the chow line, Mason looked for Casey. When they found each other, plates of food in hand, I spotted them squatting down on their helmets, hair blowing in the breeze, and shoveling down the grub. I joined them so I could hear about Mason's adventure in Hong Kong. Between mouthfuls, Mason finally chimed in, "You were so right, Casey; Charlotte was everything you said she was and more."

"Oh yeah, and more. I told you so." Casey turned to me and gave me a slight knowing smile.

29

The Spider Hole

A curve in the dirt road, a sandy embankment maybe six feet tall to the left, a rice paddy to the right, and blue skies overhead. The point man, Carl, loaded up on Darvon, spotted a black-pajama dude slipping into a spider hole just fifty meters ahead. That was how some point men rolled: wash down a few feel-good pills and take the lead. The single column of bobbing green helmets strung out behind me started bunching up.

"What do you want to do, captain?" Carl said, a bit loopy.

"Let's see if we can smoke him out," the captain responded.

"Yes, sir."

Carl obliged the captain and threw a smoke grenade into the small hole, a hole barely big enough for a gook to enter. It turns out the smoke grenade was yellow. You never know what color will come pouring out—cool.

"*Lai day.*" yelled Carl.

Typical of these situations, no response was forthcoming from the smoke-filled yellow hole. It's not like we were going to say to ourselves, "Oh, fuck it. Let's move on." Our MO was: you hide, you run away, you die. That's who we were. We were not in a no-fire zone; we weren't conferring with no village chief on whether or not we could shoot. We shot first and asked questions later. We didn't care about repercussions, 'cause there weren't none.

Another smoke grenade was tossed into the hole.

"*Lai day,* motherfucker," Carl yelled again, starting to get pissed off.

Now, I didn't rightly know whether our village dudes and dudettes knew any English cuss words, but they sure as hell could hear the urgency in Carl's voice.

"There are two spider holes," he said. "Maybe they're connected."

"Throw a smoke in both holes at the same time," the captain responded.

"Will do," Carl said.

Michael and Carl timed their throws; red started pouring out of one hole and purple out of the other. More commands. More silence.

"Fuck it, throw in a grenade," the captain ordered.

Boom! No answer.

"Throw a grenade in both holes at the same time," ordered the captain.

"Roger that."

Kaboom, and voila, pajama dude came rolling out, lifting his hands in the air—remarkable, really—mostly in good shape. Of course, his eardrums had to be destroyed.

What the fuck happened? I asked myself. *How did he escape the blast unscathed?* Not only that, how the hell could he have heard our yelling after absorbing the sound of three grenades in close quarters? Geez, it's fucking amazing what the human body can take and still keep on ticking.

"Carl, check out the spider hole," the captain ordered.

"Yes, sir," Carl answered.

Just because of Carl's small frame, he got a shit job like that: a .45 in one hand, a flashlight in the other, crawling on his belly. That was fucked up.

He was gone for what seemed an eternity, much longer than I expected.

Finally, Carl squeezed out of the entrance, brushed himself off, and reported to the captain.

"There's a girl in there. She's fucked up real bad—dead. It looks like he was using her as a shield. She took the blasts," he said while continuing to brush himself off. "Oh, and the spider holes are connected. When we doubled up on him, he had no choice."

Kit Carson—the NVA turncoat interpreter and scout, a.k.a. Fancy Pants—fashioned himself as a male model, I think. Fatigues starched and pressed, not a hair out of place, he tied a handkerchief around the gook's head, covering his eyes then tying his hands behind his back. The two men jabbered back and forth, shouting singsong sounds high and low, nothing I understood. Finally, the interpreter turned to the captain and reported, "He's a local, and the girl, she was a schoolteacher from around here." Pausing for a few seconds, he added, "I don't think he knows much, Captain."

"We'll see about that. We're shipping the son of a bitch off for interrogation." The captain turned his head my direction and ordered, "Call in the MPs."

"Yes, sir."

An hour went by, and the chopper with the MPs arrived to grab the little peckerhead. But before they took him away, the MPs, along with Fancy Pants, started in on him as I moved off a couple of meters. With the gook still blindfolded and sitting on his haunches, Kit Carson relayed the gook's version of events to the MPs—who he was, what his job was, shit like that. Fifteen minutes passed, and our prisoner, Kit, and the MPs flew off.

We were resting on top of a hill a couple of hours later when word got back to us that we'd done terrible things to him—beat him, stuck things up his ass, shit like that. "We should have crammed a number-two pencil up his ass," I said. After all, his shield lay mangled and bleeding fifteen feet inside a dark hole for the rats to feed on.

No class today. We should have killed the son of a bitch.

30

The Card Game

"When do you rotate out?" Peter asked me.

"None of your business," I said, pissed off when I drew a deuce, fucking up my straight.

The third ace landed on the green blanket covering the makeshift table—two C ration boxes, one stacked on top of the other. A poncho liner held up with bamboo over our heads worked like an umbrella, shading the action. It was midday on top of a hill at LZ Ross, everything quiet, a friendly hand of cards, getting to know the new guy, Peter. A slim, blond-haired kid, barely old enough to shave, sat opposite me and the usual suspects, except for the second lieutenant—a loud and braggadocious type and heavyset. But we liked the lieutenant anyway. I was keeping score. It was a pleasant distraction from the world around us—Ryan down twenty, Casey up forty, the lieutenant about even, the new kid down ten. I put my pencil back in my pocket after recording the last hand, closing the small green notebook. Everyone was having a good time when the mortars started falling on the other side of the hill; 105mm artillery guns were the target opposite our side. All of us knew what was going on except for the new guy. None of us said a thing; we just continued like everything was normal. The enemy were always methodical in their mortar attacks, always working in an exacting pattern. We knew it would take a few minutes to get to us but figured they'd quit before reaching the top of the hill. The target was obvious; they were after the guns and the guys feeding them.

The sound of the explosions was getting closer. Despite that, no one acknowledged the attack. I was dealt a couple of deuces. *That sucks*, I thought to myself.

"Two bucks," challenged Casey.

"I'm in," I said, knowing full well it was a dumb bet. Who knew, I might get that third deuce.

The explosions were numbering seven or eight now, and Peter finally figured out what was happening. He was too new to know when a blast was inside or outside the perimeter.

"Mortars!" screamed Peter at the top of his lungs, his head lunging forward as if someone had stomped his nut sack, like it hurts when the pain finally registers in the brain. Eyes bulging, fear written all over his face, he jumped to his feet, searching for a place to hide.

The rest of us, now sounding our internal alarms, started moving, leaving our cards on the makeshift table, hoping to finish the hand after all the hubbub. We all started for the foxhole, then realized we'd killed a bamboo viper earlier in the day and someone threw it in the hole.

"I ain't jumping in there," Casey said.

"Me neither," I said.

None of us were willing to do that. Shit, no.

"Now what do we do," Allen, the lieutenant, shouted while nervously looking for a place to hide.

"Ain't that your job, Lieutenant?" I said.

The explosions were nearing the top of the hill now, and if the gooks miscalculated somehow, we were fucked.

We spotted a row of sandbags two, maybe two and a half feet high between us and the top of the hill. We all ran over to the only option we had at this point and lay down as close as we could to the sandbags. A calculation now: if the shells started coming over the top of the hill, then we had to time it. We'd jump to the other side of the sandbag wall before the next round landed. The prospects were looking pretty shabby. We were all feeling dumb and exposed.

Silence. Sweet silence. I gave Casey a quick smile. He smiled back.

"We almost bought the farm on that one," Casey said.

Casey leaned over to Peter and said, "Welcome to the Nam."

We were all settled in for the night, the radio watch schedule in place, the mortar attack now history. Around dusk, the 3rd platoon had set up an LP—listening post—a hundred meters outside the perimeter. So, it was midnight, and this kid got up for his shift on guard duty. He was sitting there half asleep and decided to chuck a grenade from his M79 out into the bush, which was customary. Only, he forgot about the LP. The grenade sailed out into the night. *Boom!* Then a voice from the dark blared out, "YOU SON OF A BITCH, FUCKING BASTARD, CEASE FIRE, ASSHOLE!" The voices quieted in short order, and I worried someone might be injured. But then, it tickled my funny bone somehow.

31

Hot LZ

I shouted to Ryan over the helicopter blades churning overhead, "I hate being in the middle."

"Why the fuck do you care?" Ryan shouted back.

"Just do."

We were descending, making an approach to yet another landing zone, six choppers coming closer to the ground, only this time it was special. I heard a bullet puncture a hole in our tail section—a hot LZ. I pushed Ryan out of the chopper. What I didn't figure on was the eight to ten feet between the helicopter and the ground. After watching Ryan doing a beautiful somersault before landing on his butt, I followed suit. As I surveyed the area, I also didn't figure on the punji stakes—stakes planted in the dirt with sharpened tips, sometimes dipped in venomous snake poison, animal dung, or whatever nasty shit they could find. They'd planted the punji stakes all over the landing zone, but somehow we all avoided being skewered. Running for cover, careful not to engage the enemy's handiwork, we took up positions at the tree line.

"You son of a bitch," Ryan said as we took up positions.

"Yeah, well, I'd rather take my chances on the ground than be a target in the air."

"Maybe so, but you're still an asshole."

Dennis, our forward observer, was a fellow with a thin nose and eyes too close together—some might say beady—hailing from Ohio or Indiana, I didn't know and didn't care. Anyhow, he pulled out his map and started measuring shit, then grabbed the radio handset and barked in coordinates to our firebase of 105s. The first round—a white phosphorus incendiary round, leaving white smoke lingering in the air for easy visual detection—landed some distance from us. Dennis adjusted fire to bring the next round closer to our perimeter, only this time, it was of the high explosive type. It whistled down and exploded in the middle of our circular defensive perimeter. Fragments flew up and out of a shallow impression in the landscape and found no victim, leaving all of us unscathed. Dennis would have found gold if the perimeter were an archery target and the artillery round an arrow.

"Lima one point five, you stupid sons of bitches!" Dennis screamed into the handset. *"Not Romeo, over."*

A flustered Dennis fiddled with his map and instruments, adjusting fire, and then called in a dozen more rounds to suppress enemy fire. Twenty minutes passed, and after a barrage of small arms fire, our welcoming committee decided to vacate the area.

"Move out!" the captain ordered. The point man started moving west through the hilly landscape under cloudy skies, but with no threat of rain. The monsoon season made hour-by-hour forecasting impossible.

We moved out single file. As we moved along the trail's ridge, it made a tight turn to the right, exposing a rice paddy below. With Captain

Hartley a couple of meters in front of me, I noticed a farmer hoeing out in the middle of the dry rice paddy. It surprised me. Here was this guy working away, and as I raised my rifle, he finally looked up and saw me. Now in my sights, he dropped his hoe and started running for the hedge line. I moved the selector switch to full auto and asked the captain, "Should I shoot him?" He didn't answer, and I didn't pull the trigger.

The clouds gave way to blue skies and increased heat, the morning surprise party and the farmer running for his life now a memory. The afternoon was uneventful until the early evening chopper landed and unloaded ammo, mermite cans full of hot mystery meat, vegetables, bread, Korean beer, and mail. As we lined up for chow with mess kits in hand, a sergeant was nearby calling out names from the mailbag. Everything was routine until bullets rang out, piercing nearly every mermite can, hitting no one in line, making me think. Maybe the shooter had a beef with the aluminum cans—another shoot-and-run event. We fired back, and the threat vanished. Our hearts resumed their normal beat, and we settled back into our regular routine. Sitting on my butt, I shoveled in another bite of green beans and thought, *Maybe it was that farmer*. It seemed every day in the I Corps, you could count on a few enemy bullets to spice up your day, get the heart rate up, and focus your mind on the task at hand. It was like every time you thought you had it figured, some asshole came along and slapped you upside the head and told you, "You don't control shit."

Since it was still light, I started writing a letter home to the folks. I glossed over the day's events and wrote about the weather and other nonsensical stuff, revealing nothing of the mayhem confronting us.

I glanced over at Maurice, our newest RTO member in the CP, a kid from rural Maine. He had a slight build, smaller than most. With a PRC-25 radio weighing in at twenty-five pounds, and along with all the other shit we carried, he must have been struggling. The rain started falling, and he handled his first radio watch under the downpour. He looked pathetic sitting there next to the tree line with his poncho draped over his head, radio antennas reaching to the sky, all the handsets cradled in his lap. A photographer traveling with us from one of the news services snapped a photo of him. I'm sure the image encapsulated the misery of our condition.

We were all pathetic as the rain continued to come from every direction—the left, the right, overhead, down under, and sideways. It soaked everything and everybody except for those of us who safely guarded our letters with a vinyl gas mask cover. The vinyl was thick and pliable and did a fine job as the rain continued for what seemed like hours.

The next day it was off to a new location, digging foxholes and cleaning weapons. I started thinking about the shit we carried, especially the rifle. That was the one thing I took extra care of; after all, it went to bed with me every night. In the dark, it was comforting to know she was always by my side. It went with me everywhere, as if it were a part of my body—an extra appendage. Take a pee or a dump, and there it was, leaning against my leg or lying across my lap. Even though it let me down on occasion, it was the one thing I valued most.

The rain lightened up finally, and the weapons platoon lieutenant, having spotted a shed a couple of hundred meters out in the middle of a field west of us, decided to have a little fun and blow it up with a mortar—target practice, if you will. The locals probably stored their farm implements in it. The lieutenant was a proud Georgian who carried his state flag with him, making room for it in his rucksack, and when time permitted, he'd fly it from a bamboo pole. I thought it a bit counterproductive, flying bright red colors in a sea of green. But today, he challenged one of his crews to take out the shed. You might call it a morale booster, something like shooting all those water buffalo months ago. It seemed like a good idea. But for the rest of us, it was a nice distraction and we'd just see how good our mortar platoon was.

With those close by covering their ears, Chief dropped a mortar into the tube. The round slid down the tube, hitting the firing pin at the base, igniting the propellant; the round flew high, arching into the sky toward the target, then exploded about twenty feet from the shed—not bad for a first try. As Chief dropped another, then after careful adjustments another, but failed to achieve the results the lieutenant was looking for, the shed remained intact. Again, it wasn't one of our finest hours. No cheers, no celebration, just a shed mocking us as we turned our attention to other matters.

With the hour getting late, the mortar platoon prepared to fire off a few more rounds on more conventional defensive targets. Chief—I never knew his real name; we all just called him Chief—never said much, was more of a listener. He was a big man from the Navajo Nation in northeast Arizona and had no problem carrying around a twenty-five-pound baseplate or the 81mm tube. As he positioned the mortar round in the tube, he dropped it and turned to cover his ears. It was something he'd done a thousand times. Only this time was different; the round slid down the tube but failed to fire. He waited a couple of minutes to make sure it wouldn't suddenly come to life, but nothing. So, he carefully removed the tube from the legs and baseplate, picking it up with his left arm and grabbing the rim with his right hand, pointing the business end of the tube down slightly at an angle to slide the round back out. Instead of sliding out, it ignited, taking with it the fingers of Chief's right hand. There was silence, shock, then screams, then chaos, with guys dancing around like fools. Doc rushed over to administer aid, morphine, and bandages. The round dug into the dirt. Chief's fingers had probably slowed down the accelerating round from gaining the necessary force to detonate, and the medevac flew in to pick him up—another clusterfuck, another screwup, and Chief's last day in the field.

The chow and mail arrived as usual, like it was just another day, but nothing was normal.

At zero three hundred hours in the morning, the middle of the night, with the radios planted in front of me, I sat thinking about the mishaps, the bumbling events of the last couple of days: The ruined mermite cans with enemy bullets spicing up the green beans. A defiant mortar, a powwow with a chief minus four fingers—fingers that may have saved my ass—a farmer in my sights hoeing a field, and a lingering question. Should I have pulled the trigger? Would it have made a difference?

32

The Graveyard

Headstones, sand, and cactus: our home for a week. A disabled tank with a track blown off by a buried 500-pound bomb anchored the northwest corner of the graveyard—a bomb left over from an earlier airstrike turned into a booby trap. I wondered if the inhabitants of that tank had survived the blast. Probably not. I didn't ask, and I didn't want to know. Being close to the beach felt safer somehow, a welcome change from humping in the Que Son Valley. We cut bamboo poles, hammered into the sand with entrenching tools, paired our ponchos snapped together, and draped them over a crossbar. Mosquito net set, we had a place to lay our heads when night came and an armored mechanized unit to share perimeter duty. Other than sleeping on top of or beside dead people, it was going to be a good week.

Morning came soon enough with a day mission, three or four klicks from the graveyard. The choppers landed just outside the graveyard. We loaded up and started yet another adventure. Our choppers descended after a short flight to a few feet above the sand, the sand flying everywhere; we were greeted by a few local inhabitants. We couldn't see them, but we could hear the rounds they squeezed off. We were not welcome. Brushy outcroppings and tree lines surrounded the landing zone. Shouldering my M16, after clearing the blades, I fired off a round. I would have fired off more, only the bolt jammed. A grain of sand between the shell casing and the barrel chamber could ruin your whole day. So it goes with equipment failure. Luckily, we outnumbered the party poopers, and no one was worse for wear. We managed to capture a teenager an hour later. Blindfolding him and tying his hands, we guided him back to the graveyard, where our mechanized boys were set up on the south-side perimeter.

I'd picked up a nifty little camera at the PX on my way back from R & R in Taipei. A little Minolta, small enough you could slip it into your shirt pocket. Pulling on the frame would advance the 110mm film cartridge and expose the viewfinder.

Meanwhile, the captains from both our units and Kit Carson were questioning the teenager. It appeared they weren't getting the answers they wanted, so Kit slapped the kid upside the head. The kid stumbled to his left, then righted himself for the next question. From where I stood, I could barely hear the exchange. Another blow to the other side of his head, more unrecognizable gibberish. The teenager, righting himself again, stood facing the interrogator as if he could see through the handkerchief.

I was thinking, photo op. Grabbing my nifty little camera, I started snapping pics. It got uglier, and I started feeling bad for the kid. I didn't think they got all that much information, but it was the first time I'd captured that kind of shit on film. I worried the folks back in the States in the developing business would censor that kind of thing. I knew the army wouldn't approve of having shit like that plastered all over the newspaper.

The next morning I was going through my stuff and no camera. I went through my shit again and still no camera. What the fuck had happened to it? I started getting paranoid and pissed off; some motherfucker stole it while I was sleeping. How the fuck did that happen? Bastards!

Meanwhile, it was time for another patrol, time to go for a look-see. With the armor guys on the perimeter, we moved out. That's when I saw Allen Becker—a kid from back home. Imagine that, 10,000 miles away from home and running into that son of a bitch. He was a big kid, a mean bastard, held me down once when I was maybe twelve years old and held a burning cigarette to my big toenail. I didn't feel it right away, and then the pain reached my noggin. It hurt like hell. He laughed and let me go. That's the kind of kid he was. Since he was a few years older than me and one of the town's bullies, I had always avoided him as best I could. But at this chance meeting, we both smiled and exchanged pleasantries. Let bygones be bygones, so they say.

Not thirty meters from the perimeter, the invisible little peckerwoods had sneaked up during the night and placed evenly spaced bamboo sticks in the ground with propaganda fliers slid into slits in the bamboo, telling us how evil we were. I couldn't imagine how they could sneak up on us and plant those damn sticks without our knowing it. But then again, there was always something unexplainable going on.

After an hour of shuffling along, we spooked a gook trying to hide in a hedgerow. As he ran away, one of us took him down with a bullet to the knee. With the gook lying there on the ground, a Thai mercenary got to him first, outrunning the rest of us, kicking the mangled leg, screaming gibberish at him, trying to get answers before we caught up with him. We put a stop to the mercenary's activity, we still operated under the illusion that there was a code of morality in combat, that we were better than that. We may not have kicked his leg, but then again, maybe Allen's cigarette treatment to a toenail would have yielded better results. Our flamboyant Thai friend had style and a hankering to inflict pain.

THE GRAVEYARD

In early December, with Christmas just around the corner, it was our last day in the graveyard. It was time for another adventure. Time for a sweep of the sandy flat lowlands, with APCs—armored personnel carriers—along with a couple of tanks. Until now, I'd never seen either in the Nam. Ain't no tanks crawling along the jungle paths in the highlands.

The captain rounded us up, and we headed out. It felt like a WWII movie with images of army guys following General Patton's tanks across France. Images filmed during WWII, a Hollywood flick glamorizing the virtues of fucking up the enemy, floated through my brain. It had felt good somehow, as a nine-year-old, watching those Jap Zeros splashing into the ocean. I loved *Victory at Sea.* It was strange, otherworldly. Walking behind the tanks, rifle at the ready, boots sinking in the sand, trudging along, I felt like an extra on a movie set. It felt safe in a way because no self-respecting commander of enemy forces would intentionally fight us out in the open with our superior firepower. Maybe booby traps and mines, but not open warfare with our big guns and airfields close by.

The maneuver ended in disappointment. No body counts, no caches discovered, no enemy rifles to send home.

Another week in the bush, another day to mark off my eight-and-a-half-by-eleven sheet of paper. I penciled in one more piece, hoping I had time to finish. Unlike Sisyphus of mythical fame, my boulder would come to rest sooner rather than later.

33

Up in Flames

Pound cake; nothing tasted better than pound cake, even if it came out of a can. Coupled with raspberry Kool-Aid, you couldn't beat it for a little relief from the elements. I opened my mouth, elevating the treat to my lips, when the sound of gunfire filled my ears. Fuckin' gooks! An AK for sure—the sound was undeniable, and the rate of fire. Yup, an AK, and the bullets were moving from my left, creeping in my direction. Sitting on the porch of an empty pink house, I carefully placed my canteen on the ground between my boots so it wouldn't spill, screwing the lid on. I balanced the pound cake on top of the canteen, so when the attacker split, I could polish off one of my few treats.

As the bullets moved closer, it was time to make my move. Earlier, I'd eyeballed a divot to my right where I'd just lie low and wait for the opportunist to leave. What I didn't figure on was that it was too shallow. After trying to hide in the shallow hole, I jumped up and ran around to the back of the stucco house with bullets kicking up the dirt at my heels. When I rounded the corner of the house, Casey and Mason were already there.

"That fucker ain't much good at shootin' folks, is he?" Casey said.

"No shit! Damn good thing," responded Mason.

No one was hit. Thirty minutes later and Charlie's disruption was now history. There, sitting on the steps in front of the porch, was my canteen with the pound cake resting on top—it hadn't moved an inch.

Later that day, and several klicks to the north, we met up with a special Vietnamese military police unit. They were setting up camp fifty meters from us, just to the north. These weren't your typical ARVN unit. The way they acted around each other made me think they were queer. Maybe not queer, but odd and peculiar nevertheless.

It was another night in the field, only this time with a unit of wacko Vietnamese police cooking up weird shit that smelled strange. It was another first—a joint exercise to sweep the valley come sunrise.

Before the sun raised its head, everyone was milling about, getting ready for a new kind of adventure sure to be froth with excitement. It was time to move out under the dim morning light. The little police guys were impressive in their actions, getting their shit together, forming up. Efficient came to mind. Tall, spindly trees with the leaves sprouting out at the very top provided a nice canopy with equal parts green and blue sky. The police unit was there to herd the water buffalo out of the valley to a place closer to the coast. At least that's what we were told. Someone said the buffalo would be reunited with the villagers in a kind of camp for refugees—a reeducation camp of sorts. We'd dropped leaflets from a small aircraft a few days ago, telling the inhabitants they had to get their butts out of the valley. We were on a mission to burn every house, pee on every rice cache, and shoot any gook making a run for it. We were simply living up to the terms of our mission: search and destroy.

Midmorning arrived with little fanfare until a few incoming rounds broke the silence. The peaceful early morning turned to shit in a New York minute. I couldn't imagine why Charlie was all pissed off just 'cause we were fucking up their neighborhood. The bullets weren't all that close yet, but that's when that special Vietnamese police unit shifted into high gear. All I saw was the little bastards running full speed toward the fire, something totally out of character from what I'd seen in the past. It just might have been their motivation was different. They were supposed to be rounding up the water buffalo for the soon-to-be-displaced villagers, but maybe not. Who the fuck knows. All I knew was, I was fucking impressed by their bravado . . . gutsy little bastards.

I could hear gunfire getting louder as we continued along, all spread out. I lost track of the police. The peckerwoods had disappeared into the sparse vegetation like ghosts. Now the gunfire started ratcheting up, and we were stuck in the open with only the shade of the trees for cover. The spindly trees were hardly wide enough to hide behind—the landscape was flatter than a steamrolled horny toad. The urgency of the moment wasn't lost on the captain. He ordered in an air strike. There was no telling the size of the force in front of us or where the hell the police zipperheads had gone. All I knew was, the air strike couldn't get here fast enough. That's when I heard the pilot of an F-104 on the radio asking for our location. Thank God the cavalry had arrived. Wait a minute; we were the fucking cavalry. Following the roar of a screaming turbine, I could see a glimmer of silver flashing through the canopy at a fast rate of speed. A beautiful fighter jet. It was one helluva welcome sight for sure.

The first 750-lb bomb was released, arching down, dropping through the leaves, and landing not all that far in front of us. It made one hell of an impression. Following the sound, I watched the jet pull up, with the sound of AKs firing a steady stream of bullets. As I stood there watching the sky, big hunks of bomb fragments started raining down. *Ker-plunk, thud,* steel chunks landed here and there. With the force they were coming down, my fuckin' helmet was useless. And yet, there was no place to hide. I was weighing the lack of options, the pros and cons of being taken out by a hunk of steel or a bullet to the head, and coming up with no answers. After another strike, another round of white-knuckle fear, another round of steel raining down, the jets finally *di di'd*. The enemy fire stopped. I'm sure, after careful consideration of another round of the invading bombs, they decided it was time to go. Plus, there was the matter of having to drag off their dead.

We were off again to tell the villagers we encountered to vacate the premises and get out of the fucking valley.

As the sun was setting, we dug foxholes, and I pondered what the next day would bring.

The darkness took hold; sporadic gunfire started in from the northeast. It kept us awake and pinned down most of the night. Dozing off from time to time, the glow of green tracer rounds whizzing overhead, I thought it best not to take a pee lest my pecker get shot off.

As daylight emerged, the enemy either tired of shooting or exhausted their ammo supply. At any rate, due to the lack of incoming rounds, we were able to close our peepers for a short time before heading out.

I and Marvin—blue eyes, taller than me—were trudging along when we came up to a small group of houses with brick patios, mud walls, and thatched roofs. As we came to the first house, an old woman stood between me and her home. Marvin slipped in behind her and pulled out his Zippo cigarette lighter, the one Top had gotten us on his R & R trip to Japan—a gesture I appreciated even though I didn't care for the blowhard that much. It was a cool lighter with our emblem and an inscription of the year and our unit. What better use could there have been for that wonderful gesture than to flip it open, spin the wheel, and let the flame catch thatched roofs on fire? After all, we were there to destroy. And Marvin was doing a fine job.

The old lady was not so enamored of Marvin's lighter or what he did with it. A look of horror covered her face as he torched the thatched roof. The roof started slowly, then picked up steam. The old lady was grabbing a pitcher and frantically filling it with water from a giant adobe container. She struggled to lift the pitcher high enough to douse the flames. A lost cause, for sure. She'd managed to throw a single pitcher full of water onto the flames when Marvin took the butt of his rifle and broke the large water reservoir. Like a cracked eggshell, the water started seeping, then flowing freely through the cracks and fissures. The old woman stood there with an empty pitcher, her mouth gaping, tears at the corners of her eyes, looking at the flames, then at the reservoir, and back again at the burning roof. Powerless, she stood there as we kept moving. Gone was her altar to worship her ancestors, along with everything else. It was on to another house, another opportunity, another roof to light up.

As the day wore on, more villagers of all ages followed us across the valley, keeping pace and crying, the sounds of torment echoing in my ears. We were like the pied piper of destruction. I was having trouble coming to grips with the situation. There must have been a hundred trailing us, stretching a quarter mile, carrying nothing with them except for a baby here and there. When I turned my head to look at the long line, a woman not far away stood out; her face reminded me of a mask, the frowny theater mask out of a Greek tragedy, a contorted mouth. Why would they do that? Why would they follow the ones who torched their homes and peed on their rice? What was up with that? Why didn't they leave when we told them to? After all, we'd dropped those pamphlets from the air a week ago. I looked over at Marvin and said, "Don't they know what's good for them?" Marvin said nothing, and I don't suppose he cared.

UP IN FLAMES

A couple of days later, the villagers were supposedly off to a camp on the coast somewhere, reunited with their buffalo. I questioned whether that ever happened. I figured the Vietnamese military police unit wasn't so willing to give them up.

It was foxholes and hooches for another night in no-man's-land with booby traps and unwanted neighbors prowling about in the darkness. With the valley free of civilians, someone in command figured it was time to call on Puff the Magic Dragon, a.k.a Spooky—an AC-47 gunship. It was a slow-flying plane with an open door allowing a mini-gun to fire hundreds of rounds a second of 7.62 ammo. Sitting on the ground in front of my hooch, I realized why it was called Spooky: as it circled the area north of us, the bullets raining down from the doorway like a whip, the red tracers were almost continuous, fluid, like a fire-breathing dragon tearing up the ground below. It was surreal, like the B-52 strike. When the show ended, I hoped it would keep the wolves at bay long enough to get a few hours of uninterrupted sleep.

34

Body Bags

There we were, setting up camp at the base of the mountain, the rain coming down hard, running down my backside as I bent over to drive in a stake. Unbeknownst to us was a figure with a poncho over his head, looking down at the dike separating two rice paddies, his AK slung over his shoulder, placing one foot carefully in front of the other on the slick wet mud. He lifted his head to check out an unfamiliar sound. When he spotted us, and we spotted him, he panicked. I don't think he heard our shouting, he just ran. M16s opened up on both sides of me, the bright red magnesium-filled tracers burning, piercing his poncho then disappearing into his body. Yet, he kept running. In fact, he quickened his pace like a tightrope walker does, finishing his last few steps to safety, his body filling with lead, never losing balance, moving along the slippery dike then around a mound of dirt. Then he was gone; the son of a bitch ran plum out of sight. I couldn't believe my eyes.

Of course, we went looking for him. Yeah, he made it out of sight, all right, but only about fifty meters. He lay on his right side, slipped off the high wire, finished. Here he was, diddy-bopping along in the rain and cold, and then we came along and fucked up his whole day. We rummaged through his belongings for intel, then left him lying there for his buddies. They were pretty good about policing their dead.

Radio communication from Battalion informed us that Bravo Company was in a world of shit nine or ten klicks away and that choppers were on their way to pick us up.

By the time we arrived at the new location, the gunfire had ceased, except for a few sporadic shots here and there from the direction of where Bravo Company was engaging with the enemy.

Sitting cross-legged near some vegetation shielding me from the setting sun, the shadows of the mountain range soon to take over, I was cursing the heat and the Que Son Valley when a gook emerged from the mouth of the ravine at a slow trot. Carlos spotted him first.

"*Lai day,* motherfucker!" Carlos, a Puerto Rican, shouted. Carlos was proud, self-assured, and a damn good fighter—he didn't back down from nothing.

When the little bastard heard the command and looked up, he had twenty rifles pointed in his direction. He dropped his rifle and raised his hands.

Looking over at Mason, I said, "At least this one was smart enough to stop."

The runner had an attack plan for a Vietcong division to our south. Shit like coordinating times, locations, and logistics.

"Wow, that can't be good," I said. "What's worse, two divisions are coming down this canyon later tonight. And if we don't get our butts out of here, we're toast."

"Fuckin' A, roger that," Mason agreed.

We were a long way from base camp, and Bravo Company was already gone. Half of our company had choppered out thirty minutes ago, and I worried the chopper pilots might think it too risky to return since it was getting dark. From what we could tell from the documents the runner was carrying, the lead elements of two NVA divisions could appear at the mouth of the ravine at any moment. I imagined they'd be like a swarm of killer bees pissed off at us for smacking around one of their own. There was no telling how much time we had. Fifty against hundreds, maybe a thousand: now we were the ones perched on the high wire waiting on a lifeline, a safety net.

Looking into the sky, no birds in sight, I listened hard for the sound of blades dicing up the air—a chatter. That distinctive sound only a Huey can make. Two NVA divisions would break out into the open at any moment, the ravine full of hundreds of assholes carrying RPGs, AKs, satchel charges, mortars—every fuckin' thing a division could carry was coming our way. With the sun sliding farther down the far side of the mountain, I started thinking maybe they wouldn't come back, that I should have left on the first sortie. Then I heard the most beautiful sound in the world, the faint clap of a blade, then another, then a crescendo of blades. Beautiful.

Landing on LZ Leslie, knowing the shit was going to hit the fan sooner than later, I got the crew working on wiring the bunkers with phones. You can never have enough communication in a shitstorm. Tensions were high, knowing the little peckerheads were probably lurking just outside the concertina wire. Stringing communications wire from one bunker to the next, we tested connections. Being pressured by the foreboding night sky had my stomach in knots. This time it wasn't like in the past when the bullets would fly and we were surprised by an ambush.

You know when a UPI photographer hangs out with you hoping to catch some action. You know when a major general comes out to apologize for not getting you back to base camp for almost a year because he didn't have the troops to relieve you. You know when a reporter sticks a microphone in your face wanting to know, "What's it like out there?" When Westmoreland rides around your base camp eyeballing the troops, climbs back into his helicopter, and disappears: you know the action is not far off. With puckered assholes all around, it felt like a boxing match with round one about to begin and all of us in the ring hanging out in our respective corners. We knew we'd be on the ropes getting pummeled to start but were hoping for a knockout before the final bell. Soon, with the enemy's clock ticking down, careers would be made; lives would be spared, ruined, or wasted when the enemy's mallet struck the bell.

It was a late night; with all the phones operational, it was time for some shut-eye. Come morning, lying peacefully on my air mattress, sleeping under my poncho liner in the early morning hours, I felt a sudden pain in my right foot. Then another, awaking me out of a sound sleep. What the fuck, someone was kicking my foot.

I heard the words, "Get up, get up, time to get your lazy ass up and at 'em, soldier."

Sudden rage filled my body. Who the hell was kicking my foot? With a fuzzy mind and intense anger, I reached down along the left side of my air mattress and grabbed a Colt .45 handgun—the one Erickson had been tired of carrying and loaned me. I pulled back on the slide and chambered a round; I pointed the pistol in the direction of my feet at the mouth of the hooch. As my eyes focused, I didn't see the asswipe's feet, legs, or face, nothing but blue skies. The voice finally registered in my brain. I knew it was the first sergeant. And I didn't give a shit even if it was God almighty. You don't fuck with my feet. I scooted out of the hooch, and Top was nowhere around. An hour went by, and Top came up behind me as I was looking out over the concertina wire and marveling at the beauty of the rice paddies, the morning light, the patterns created by the dikes reflecting water, the terracing of the valley, and all the shades of green, so peaceful.

"Are you OK?" he asked.

"I'm fine."

"Just wanted to make sure you're all right."

"No, I'm fine. You just surprised me, is all."

"OK," he said after a moment of contemplation.

He stood next to me, staring off into the distance for a few more minutes, neither of us saying a word. He turned and left.

With all the bunkers wired now, I sat down to clean my rifle, then reread a letter from Marilyn. I'd never met her in the flesh, but she'd sent a color photo of herself in a dress. She had brown hair and a pleasant smile. Mason had told her about me and thought she might want to write to me. Who knew, if I made it out of this shit, maybe I'd look her up someday. She lived on the east side of the San Francisco Bay in San Leandro.

Around sixteen hundred hours, orders came down from Battalion: most of us were flying back to Ross, leaving a platoon to help Delta Company guard the perimeter. It seemed odd to split up the company like that, but who knows why or how decisions are made. At the last minute—just before the choppers lifted off—Top ordered me to go with him. It seemed like a spur-of-the-moment thing, but I welcomed the order.

I stepped onto the ground at Ross—a much bigger LZ. There was a weird feeling. Something in the air was unsettling, a nervousness like on Leslie—the valley lousy with NVA. The hour was getting late, and

Dennis started calling in defensive artillery from LZ Leslie. Fumbling with the map, wiping the sweat from his brow, a drop of sweat falling off the end of his rather thin nose, he keyed the handset and ordered, *"Fire for effect, over."* The trick was to get the rounds to hit as close as possible to the perimeter without blowing up our guys.

Our command post was fifty meters or so inside the perimeter, a decent-sized bunker with sandbag walls, steel rails holding up a sandbag roof, an entranceway protected by a sandbag wall. It was big by bunker standards. It could easily accommodate seven or eight guys. The rest of the company was on the line protecting the south and southwestern ends of the base. Other companies took care of the rest.

Larry, the little queer guy who'd hit on me a few weeks back, was on radio watch in the bunker. We were facing the southern perimeter, all the radios and handsets lying on a makeshift table. Everything was going along swimmingly. Everything was sighted in; all of us were feeling good, ready for whatever was coming our way. That is, until I heard the speaker from within the bunker explode. LZ Leslie was firing a few extra rounds, making sure their guns were positioned correctly.

Entering the bunker, I spotted Larry holding the handset away from his ear.

"The shells are landing inside the perimeter, god damn it!" screamed the 3rd platoon lieutenant over the company net.

"Check fire, check fire, over!" the lieutenant continued frantically.

Larry started in. *"Cool it, man. Calm down. Don't sweat it, man. It'll be all right. I'll take care of it, over."* I could tell the little bastard was loaded up on wacky weed, higher than a kite. I ordered him out as the lieutenant kept screaming for action. Can't say I blamed him. I radioed to check fire. Even though the rounds were exploding inside the perimeter, there were no injuries—a fucking miracle. Fucking Larry, I should have bitch-slapped the little bastard.

"Dodged a big one there, didn't we," I said to Mason. The FO,

Dennis, was still pissed off at the crew back on Leslie for fucking up the coordinates they had worked on earlier.

Darkness and silence fell. The night brought the unknown. It was so dark I could hardly see my hand in front of my face. Yet, how is it that nothing stops the other guy from taking advantage when it's so dark? Puzzling. While I was still on radio watch, our guys on the south end of the perimeter started receiving gunfire. It's weird, we'd be throwing grenades all night and still sleep like babies. But the first noise out of the ordinary and it was balls to the wall, our eyes bugged out like a freshly smashed toad.

"Return fire," I could hear someone shouting. The tranquility of a few minutes ago turned to shit. Then more gunfire; it seemed like it was coming in from all directions. The lieutenant on the south perimeter called for artillery. The battery on LZ Leslie started chucking 105mm shells our way. Behind me, I heard the sound of our guns firing, the artillery shells crisscrossing high in the dark sky, looking for enemy targets at both LZs. It was what we'd all feared a few days ago when we interrogated the NVA runner. The enemy was ringing the bell.

The artillery shells kept coming as close to the perimeter as possible. But the explosions from both friendly and enemy fire were landing inside and outside the wire now: illumination rounds floating high above, bullets whistling through the air, everyone scrambling around trying to figure out their next move. Rockets started flying in, creating more havoc, leaving holes big enough to blow our shit away if one of them happened to hit our bunker. Enemy mortar shells were falling everywhere. My asshole was tighter than a Scotsman's wallet.

As the assault continued, everyone in the bunker now, we started to fear the doorway. If the gooks were inside the wire, they could be showing up at our doorway anytime. Nothing like a satchel charge blowing up in your face. That's when Larry—we forgot about Larry—decided it was safer in the bunker. The fucker must have been really confused after all that weed and fireworks. He rounded the corner of the bunker opening with more than one rifle pointed in his direction, ready to pull the trigger. Lucky for him, we hesitated just long enough for him to escape certain death.

The rest of the night we maintained our position as the bullets, rockets, grenades, artillery rounds, PRGs—you name it—went off.

Light on the horizon. It was morning, and the aftermath of the night was everywhere, like awaking from a deep sleep after having dropped acid—everything weird, zombies milling about, lifeless facial expressions, eyes searching for nothing in particular. The enemy dragging off their dead and wounded—like they always do. Yeah, there were some hanging in the wire, but for the most part, they were gone. We'd managed to keep them at bay. Helicopter gunships circled the area, counting bodies, keeping score.

LZ Leslie wasn't so lucky with gooks inside the wire.

Top, the captain, Ryan, Mason, and I flew out to Leslie to check on our guys. Top was full of concern; you could see it in his eyes as he surveyed the carnage, asking the ones still breathing if they were OK. Even though I thought he was full of shit, he had moments where his humanity shined through.

I sat down on the ground next to Marco, the platoon radio operator; he acknowledged my presence then shifted his eyes back to the horizon. Sitting on the ground, he started in: "The fuckers zipped through our wire like it was Swiss cheese. The first guy used wire cutters, the next guy ran up to our bunker and threw in a satchel charge, and the third one fired his rifle in support. Fucking unbelievable precision and timing. The satchel charge stunned us and then the little peckerheads climbed up on top of the bunker and ate our C rations. I could hear them laughing, speaking gibberish. Man, it was weird; they had to have been stoned. Why they didn't throw in a grenade and finish the job, I'll never know."

"That's fucked up, man," I said lamely.

"Yeah, weird," he said, with his eyes searching for something in the distance.

After sitting in silence, looking around, trying to absorb the moment, imagining the terror of a few hours ago, Marco continued.

"Yeah, we loaded up Robert, Charles, and Dewey." Hesitating a moment, he then added, "And Ron." They probably got wasted early on. We hadn't been able to get to them until a few hours ago. There were dead fuckers everywhere. Our guys were probably zipped up in body bags by now. I didn't know about the artillery and the Delta Company guys or how many they lost. A lot of them got fucked up, too.

The same shock back at Ross felt even more profound here. We hadn't been overrun yet. These poor bastards had been helpless. What do you do, play dead and hope they pass you by?

Marco continued. "I don't know when the gooks left. I know it was still pretty dark . . . but getting light." He pointed to the east at a sort of enclave. "Six of the bastards were pinned against the wall over there trying to get around the corner; they knew they were fucked." Looking over and following the direction his finger was pointing, I understood the situation. With the sun coming up, they had nowhere to go. "They waited too long. It was like shooting fish in a barrel. You can see them over there all fucked up. They tried to surrender. One of them was waving a little white flag of sorts—the wacky weed a distant memory, sobered up, they were out of ammo. They got what they deserved," Marco said. There was something in his telling that felt wrong—something that went against his core, his sense of fair play, maybe. Everyone had been dealt a shitty hand.

Top asked for a volunteer to ID our KIAs. He needed a witness to sign the death notices—someone who knew 'em. I figured what the hell, it'd get me out of here for a day or two. Top acted a little surprised when I volunteered, but he accepted my volunteering. Top and I boarded a chopper headed for Chi Lai.

It was sunny and bright in the ever-present heat, and we landed close to the command tent. Top looked at me and said, "You'd better stay out here while I find out what the score is."

Checking my watch, I saw it was twenty minutes before Top came back out and informed me, "The colonel wants you on guard duty."

What was up with that? I was here to ID my guys, and the SOB put me on guard duty. No NCO club, no beer, just a fucking night in the sandbag Hilton.

"Sorry about that," Top continued.

I believed him. He was a bit of a sycophant, like some first sergeants, willing to blow the old man if he was so inclined.

Making my way over the soft sand out to the bunker, I saw two guys—desk jockeys during the day and pretend warriors at night—sitting there, staring out through the opening of the bunker, looking nervous. You could tell guard duty wasn't their idea of a good time. And once they found out who I was, a grunt, a combatant with a bad attitude, pissed off at their fucking commander, I'm sure their sphincters tightened a bit more.

It wasn't an hour, and I noticed Top trudging across the sand, headed our way. The two guys in the bunker with me started getting nervous, wondering what the hell a first sergeant was doing checking on them.

Top called me out and explained out of earshot of the others that he'd tried hard to get me out of this but got overruled. It started me thinking that it was mighty nice of him to apologize. Then I wondered if it had anything to do with the pistol I'd pulled on him. Why was he so nice when he could have had me court-martialed?

Morning arrived without fanfare. There was chow time, then the task at hand. The technician pulled the canvas flap of the morgue open so Top and I could enter. Death filled the air and dim lights lit the walls; a row of containers lined one wall. ID info on labels identifying the dead residents perfectly aligned as if in formation, spaced correctly. Only now they lay in the prone position, at ease for eternity.

The technician pulled on the handle and slid the first body out, laying it on a tray. Grabbing the zipper on the body bag, he pulled it halfway down and parted the bag to expose the head so I could get a good look. The sliver of gold in Dewey's left front tooth caught my eye under the dim lights, making it shine. If it hadn't been for the tooth, there was no way I could have ID'd him. As for the others, I struggled to make sense of the contorted faces; rigor mortis rendered them almost unrecognizable. Signing my name on the witness papers, for their remains to be sent to the right place back in the world, I asked myself what I'd gotten myself into. One by one, the heavy zippers were pulled up snug. Then, one by one, they were slid into the vault awaiting transport. As I glanced back at the wall, I thought of the family and friends that would gather and have a service, the notice posted in the local newspaper, and finally the body laid six feet under, another nineteen-year-old, trained up, sent to war, and memorialized with a snapshot on the family mantel.

The roar of the chopper engine started spinning up, the blades whooshing faster and faster. I climbed up and sat next to Top. It was thirty minutes back to LZ Ross with early morning clear skies. The monsoons, the incessant rains were hiding for a spell. Then I started thinking about the guys back in Dak To laid out nicely on the ground. This was different somehow, odd. Maybe it was signing my name on the piece of paper. Crossing off a bureaucratic box, a formality as if to say, "Ole George is in bag number three. Make sure he gets back to Georgia." Looking at me, Top thanked me for helping him out and asked if there was anything he could do for me.

"Yeah, I'd like to go on leave," I answered. I'd thought about the answer for a split second and went for gold. What did I have to lose?

"Where do you want to go?"

"Japan." I'd never been there. I couldn't believe he took me seriously.

"I'll fix up the paperwork."

Helluva thing, trying to figure out who was who in a dim-lit morgue. Guys I was walking around with a couple of days ago were flying back home and I was off to Japan. Wine, women, and fancy chow: it pays to stay alive.

35

Leaving for An Khê

Bennington, the clerk handling the paperwork, typing orders, filing, communicating with Battalion over personnel matters and other details as ordered by his superiors, was a Midwesterner with a pleasant personality and the smarts to know how to handle himself when communicating with a bunch of crazies fresh from the field. He was sitting behind his metal desk, darkness settling in for the night; he looked up when I entered. Although he was expecting me, it surprised him as I took a quick look around. It was just the two of us in the company headquarters orderly room. I could see he was upset with the news coming from the field over the radio.

"What's happening? What's going on?" I asked.

"A Chinook was shot down outside of LZ Ross," Bennington said. Then he added, "Major Williams, the XO, was on board. I don't know who else. Charlie shot it down a couple of klicks from Ross, fell fifty feet out of the sky from what I understand." Then he continued, "The colonel choppered out a couple of companies to rescue the survivors. From what I can tell, the situation turned to shit from there. The whole valley was filled with gooks. Surrounded."

"How long ago?" I asked.

"About three hours ago," Bennington answered. "As of now, only half of them made it back, from what I can tell. Maybe more by now."

I stared over at our guidon, a flag pinned to the wall behind him—red over white, with our unit numbers and crossed rifles—and said, "That's fucked up, man."

The SIT-REPs continued from LZ Ross, Bennington paying close attention.

Sitting on the little metal chair in the corner of the orderly room, I was thinking, if I hadn't pulled that pistol on the first sergeant, I'd be right in the thick of it.

Between field reports, Bennington gave me the lay of the land: where to sleep, where the armory was to turn in my rifle . . . the usual stuff you needed to know. Base camp was different from months back. Now we shared An Khê with the 173rd Airborne. I wasn't sure how the commanders had carved this place up, but the Airborne had their piece of the pie, and we had ours. Not a good idea to cross those invisible lines. It was a turf thing, protecting your own.

"Thanks," I said, and left.

I thought to myself as I sat on the end of my bunk, *I could have been there. I should have been there. Fuck, and Major Williams was with them.* The image of him filtered through my mind again. Most likely, no one survived the crash. Major Williams, the battalion executive officer, always made a point of checking on me, asking how I was doing. I really liked that man—a sincere, no-bullshit officer like Captain Carter and Captain Hartley. They don't make them any better than that. And then, he gets shot down in a fucking Chinook.

After checking in all my shit with the E-6—the rear echelon asshole, the one responsible for operations in the rear—it was beer time. It was a new club to me, with knotty pine walls, a long bar, tables, and chairs surrounding a western band playing in the corner. Was it even real? The fellow handling bar duties set a cold glass of beer on the pinewood bar. The sweat beads forming on the glass were something I hadn't seen in a long time. Then the first sip, a reminder of a world out of my reach for months, went down smooth and refreshing. The need for a warm beer or two at the end of the day was history now.

I was on my second beer now, and I heard a 175mm artillery round fired off from somewhere on the perimeter. I was used to the 105s, but the 175mm round made a lot more noise. Instincts kicked in, and I ran out of the bar with the country-western band still playing, not missing a beat. And there I was, lying on the ground covering my head. It took a second to realize I was the only dumbass in a prone position out under a tree. I looked back in the bar, and the two guys sitting next to me still had beers in hand and were staring at me like I was some sort of freak. Not saying a word, I walked back in, sat down, grabbed my beer, and took another swig.

It was no cause for celebration; my mind was still reflecting on the crash and my guys sneaking through enemy lines in the dark. How many of my comrades were going to make it back to camp and survive yet another battle? How many?

"Another beer," I called to the bartender.

After too many beers, walking the best I could back to the barracks, I found my assigned bunk and passed out.

The next day, waiting on orders to Japan, I walked up to the main road that led to the Red Cross center. As the trucks and jeeps moved along at the base of the mountain to the north, the dust and smell of black diesel exhaust filled my nostrils. I killed a little time drinking coffee and touching a bit of the world by thumbing through the pictures in *Look* and *Life* magazines. Maybe I'd even visit with one of the round-eyed girls wearing light blue dresses managing the place. Other than the UPI photographer, I hadn't seen a Western girl in months. The photographer was a puzzle to me. What made a woman volunteer to photograph war up close and personal? I was wondering where she did her business in the bush when a couple of assholes rolled up in their jeep and yelled, "Hey, grunt, get off the road!" My hands flinched, grabbing air, but my rifle was gone, locked up. At that exact moment in time, I realized why the army had such things as armories, why they took my rifle away. Anger swelled like an uncontrollable torch, my neck burning from the fire and heat. They had no right to call me a grunt, to disrespect me or my kind. My guys could call me whatever they liked, but these sum-bitches deserved a bullet to the head.

At the center, lounging in a comfortable chair, I pulled out the piece of paper with the helmet and boots. I fished out the ballpoint pen from my pocket and inked in another day.

"What are you doing?" asked a woman named Sharon. At least that's what her name badge said.

"It's a sheet of paper where you can count down your last hundred days. Like a puzzle."

"May I see it?" She asked. "Interesting. Thanks for sharing," she said, then added, "Not many days to go."

"Nope."

I folded it up and put it back in my paperback book, using it as a marker.

Coffee and small talk just weren't doing it for me anymore. Sharon was nice and all, but it felt awkward. Like there was a distance I couldn't span. Fuck *Reader's Digest*, *Look*, and *Life;* I made my way back the mile or so to the company area.

I walked into the orderly room to see what news Bennington might have from Ross. The door swung open, and Jerry, from the 3rd platoon, scuffled in, black hair flying high above his head in the usual unwieldy way and looking all fucked up, totally batshit crazy. His mannerisms, the way he looked at you, he wasn't right. It was getting dark outside, my mood in the shitter.

"How you doing, man?" I asked. "What's happening out there?"

"Same old shit," Jerry said, dismissing the recent reports without looking at me. Bennington laid out the routine for him. Directions to the barracks, chow hall, armory, etc. He grabbed his shit and left.

That wasn't like the guy I'd spent the last year humping the bush with.

"Hey, Bennington, Jerry looks all fucked up in the head. What do you think is wrong with him?"

"Nothing. All you assholes look like that when you get out of the field. What the hell do you think you looked like a few days ago? It just takes a little time."

It was another night of drinking. The bar closed at the usual hour, and I stumbled back to the barracks. Finding my bunk in the dim night light, I pulled back the blanket and sheet and laid my head down.

Kaboom! A fucking grenade woke me out of my drunken state, like someone had stuck a firecracker up my ass. The barracks exploded with activity—guys jumping down from the top bunk, others pulling up their pants—and an unintelligible noise screamed through the night.

"The lieutenant's been hit!" a voice announced.

The lieutenant had been aiming his pecker at the piss tube stuck in the ground outside the barracks when someone tossed a grenade in his direction.

"Someone blew up the goddamn lieutenant!" the voice continued.

Someone flipped on the lights, and the others went to investigate and aid the lieutenant. The sergeant called a formation to restore some semblance of order. Five of us volunteered to go after whoever pulled the pin on the grenade. It took some considerable persuasion, but he agreed to open up the armory, allowing us to get our rifles so we could hunt down the peckerwood who did it.

A noise from the chow hall alerted us. No one should be in the chow hall at this time of night. Immediately, we spread out with guns at the ready to fuck up whoever was in there. Bursting through the doors, we searched down the rows of tables and every nook and cranny—nothing.

In my drunkenness, I asked the staff sergeant if I could go out into the tall elephant grass and get the bastard. My state of mind was such that it was time to kill something or someone. Particularly because it was one of our guys that got blown up. It didn't matter to me if it was one of us or a gook. I wanted to put him down.

The staff sergeant tried to talk sense to me. "If you go out there, how will we know if it's you and not some gook stumbling around?"

In my foggy mind, it started to make sense. What was I, a fucking nutjob? To answer my own question: yeah, pretty much.

A couple of days later, orders in hand, I was on a C-130 to Cam Ranh Bay. With a short-sleeve uniform and cunt cap, money in my wallet, a boner at the ready, it was time to take leave of this hellhole.

Cam Ranh Bay was beautiful except for the plumes of black smoke billowing from the fifty-five-gallon drums cut in half—diesel fuel, shit, and some poor bastard stirring the concoction. It was the only distraction other than the concertina wire from the otherwise beautiful white sandy beach. Even with the whiffs of burning shit drifting through the air, I would have traded places with these lucky bastards any day. The rumor was, some of them had even obtained surfboards.

That night I stationed myself in one of the base clubs. A Korean band was performing American rock and roll classics with go-go girls— Korean style with skimpy outfits barely covering their butt cheeks. The beer flowing freely, I thought to myself, *I could get used to this*. At one point, nature being what it is, I had to bleed my lizard. In the head, urinals lined the pinewood wall, everyone's wangers in full view of the asshole peeing next to you. One of the assholes with the same patch on his shoulder as me (1st Cav) sidled up next to me.

"What unit are you with?" asked the asswipe.

When I told him, he pinched his pecker midstream, buttoned his fly, and moved off in a hurry. It dawned on me. Given the treatment we got back in base camp, we had a reputation—crazy motherfuckers. We hadn't been to base camp as a unit for almost a year. All the reports, the rumor mill, must have told stories of our exploits. Six months ago, when I went back to base camp for R & R, we would get a certain amount of disrespect from the office personnel and other base camp types. But now, we were all a bunch of crazy motherfuckers capable of going gonzo at any minute. I kind of enjoyed the rep.

36

Japan

Hector Ortega, a Marine, sat next to me. We had something exceptional in common. Remarkable. When you thought about it, we both had been granted leave from a combat zone. No one gets leave from a war zone.

"How could we be so lucky?" I asked Hector.

"I don't know, man."

"Whereabouts were you?" I asked.

"Up near the DMZ." He paused a few seconds, then added, "How about you?"

"Que Son Valley," I said while thumbing through the airline magazine.

"Why do you think they let us go on leave?" I continued.

Hector started in. "I don't know, man. Things got pretty fucked up out there for me."

"For me, too," I added.

Then Hector added, "Maybe 'cause my squad got ambushed, fucking NVA were everywhere. I was the squad leader. All my guys got wasted," he mumbled, then paused.

I didn't say a word.

"I was the only survivor," he added.

After being quiet for a moment, the jet engines roaring, I said, "That's fucked up, man."

"Without a scratch, man. It fucked me up bad. I figure my captain thought I'd gone Looney Tunes, that I needed to get out of that hellhole for a day or two."

I was surprised by his forwardness, laying out the guilt he felt to someone he hardly knew. We hit it off somehow, maybe because we'd shared the chaos of battle, the blood, living on the edge of insanity. Unlike me, who'd received the summons from President Johnson to report for duty, Hector had volunteered. In both cases, the unwritten status read "expendable." For me, it was either go to prison or go to hell. It wasn't that Hector didn't believe in the mission; he was a dutiful warrior, as was I when the shit hit the fan. Although Hector volunteered, being a Marine and all, no one in their right mind signs up to watch his buddies get blown away, the guys you relied on to save your butt, who laughed at your stupid jokes, who listened to your triumphs and confessions.

Landing in Tokyo surprised me; it was modern. Neon lights were everywhere I looked, like Las Vegas. But it was cold, freezing . . . fucking short-sleeve khaki uniforms. We were jungle refugees, misfits in a foreign land in January. But then I thought, on the bright side, it was a new adventure, minus the bullets.

The short transport van motored along the streets in the left lane, the driver on the wrong side of the front seat. "What's up with that?" I said to myself. The Tokyo lights were in the rearview mirror now; we were on our way to Yokohama. It reminded me of Southern California, where you can't tell one city from another. The darkness of the windy, tree-lined road lay in front of us, the headlights illuminating it. Yes, another adventure, another hotel, another lounge full of liquor, hookers, and pimps. Who made these arrangements, anyhow? What did the military do? Call up the Japanese embassy and say: "We need a nice hotel close to Tokyo International stocked with a hundred—no, make that two hundred hookers, just enough pimps to keep them in line, and a well-stocked supply of liquor. Oh, and make sure they're clean. We don't want to police up a bunch of diseased dicks since they're needed back at work in a week."

We grabbed our shit and disembarked the transport for the bright lights of the lobby. From what I could tell, the army had done a commendable job of negotiating the terms of whatever agreement they made. Upscale came to mind. The long parkway was filled with rows of trees and grass, with large hotels facing the manicured dead winter grass, high on a hill overlooking the city. Sure enough, it was full of businesspeople and a few finely dressed pimps ready to offer up flesh and other items of interest at a reasonable price. Like in Taipei, the women weren't on display in the typical fashion, as in the whorehouses outside Tigerland back in Louisiana.

After checking in, I got the key to the room and made my way to the stairwell, where the desk clerk directed us; that was where Mr. Opportunity lined the wall with young ladies—Oriental pleasure against the wall on every step.

"What's your room number?" Mr. Opportunity asked while following me up the stairs. I told him, realizing we were on display, too, as we ascended the stairs. Pretty clever, I figured. John Q. Public wouldn't be any the wiser. The matchmaker took care of the details, figured who went with whom, and that was that. I thought it was a bit like the army. You don't get to choose. Oh, you can refuse a girl, but then what?

I got my shit out on the dresser and started checking the amenities when the knock on the room door sounded. As I opened the door, I saw a young lady wearing a lovely dress with a colorful pattern of big, swirling stripes—a bit more Westernized than what I'd seen in Taipei.

"Hello, my name is Michiko," she said from the doorway, then paused.

"Come in, come in," I said.

After an awkward couple of moments and a short discussion of services, we had an agreement with the terms. It was time for the business at hand. Michiko ran a bath—a small square tub filled with hot water. As I undressed and stepped into the water, I found it was hotter than hell. I'd figured she wanted to scald the shit out of the ringworm on my infected hand and whatever else I'd brought with me from the jungle. The one thing it did do was relax the hell out of me—something I'd not experienced in months. There was just a shower in the hotel room in Taipei, and no tubs in Vietnam. A fucking luxury, that's what it was.

After services were rendered, I asked, "Where can I pick up some supplies—a toothbrush, deodorant, shit like that—and something to drink?"

"They have a gift shop in the lobby, and there's a bar on the top floor."

"Great!" Feeling almost human, I took the elevator down with Michiko to take a look around. A walk on the promenade would be nice—stretch the legs, breathe some night air—if only it weren't so fucking cold.

I noticed a tall bottle of saki at the gift shop when we came in, then a beer vending machine; you'd never see that in the States. It seemed a bit weird.

"Let me grab a bottle of that saki," I said to Michiko as we entered the gift shop. Geez, it was late.

After I purchased the supplies, Michiko excused herself—said she had to go and would meet me tomorrow afternoon. Unlike in Taipei, I wouldn't see her until the next day. That was the deal, I guess, here in Japan. That was all right, though; I wanted to spend a little time by myself.

I took the bottle of saki, the toothpaste, the deodorant, etc., up to my room. Since the bar was still open on the top floor, I took the elevator to get a drink. A curly-haired kid sitting at the bar, a kid I recognized from the flight, looked up as I grabbed the stool next to him. "Mind if I sit here?" Another fellow was on the other side of him, a kid with a round, fat face. Looking up at the menu, I started reading: Sidecar, Pink Lady, Stinger. The bartender, dressed in a white shirt, white sweater, and black bow tie, asked what I wanted. "Beer, whatever you have on tap." Below the menu on the wall were US military patches: 4th Infantry, 101st Airborne, and some I didn't recognize.

The three of us decided to grab a table.

The lights were dim; the music on the jukebox was American pop music. In the field, music was nonexistent, except for the time the door gunner yanked my shirt's sleeve during an air assault and handed me his helmet. With earphones turned up loud, I could hear Donovan singing "Universal Soldier," a protest song written by Buffy Sainte-Marie. The lyrics described a soldier as coming from every walk of life and religion using every kind of instrument of war throughout history, and claimed that if it wasn't for people like me, there would be no more war. As if any of us could say, I ain't going.

And now, there were no guns, no chopper blades slicing through the air, no grenades going off in the distance. Strange indeed.

"Has anyone seen Hector?" I asked. "He's the Marine I flew next to on the way up here."

"No, I haven't seen him since we got settled in," Curly said.

"I ain't seen him either," the round-faced boy from Georgia said in his Southern drawl.

"I expect he'll show up for breakfast," I said.

We had a few more drinks, and I decided to turn in.

"Catch you later."

The next morning I had breakfast on the hotel's top floor, with a view to the south of the promenade below; across the way, a building looked strangely out of place, like something out of Bavaria. The hotel restaurant had Formica tables covered with white linen and chromed steel chairs with Naugahyde seats and backrests, white booths positioned just so. All the young waitresses had short hair and blue dresses trimmed with white collars and white aprons.

As I entered the room, I spotted Curly and the Georgia boy sitting at a booth and smiled. After negotiating the tables and chairs, I sat down.

"I saw your buddy last night," Curly said. "At least, I think it was him. I couldn't tell for sure, but he was one fucked-up dude. He was out on the promenade, screaming and hollering, jumping around doing crazy shit."

"Yeah, but you're not sure?" I asked.

"I don't know, man. It sure looked like him."

"What happened?" I asked.

"Some MPs showed up and hauled his butt away," Curly said. "Looking out my window, watching the MPs chasing him down was freaky. He was just running, jumping, screaming, a complete nutjob."

Poor bastard, I thought.

I figured the locals had called the MPs, and that he wound up in a psych ward. He'd probably never make it back to the Nam, or the world, for that matter. None of us would make it back, I thought, not with any semblance of sanity.

The one thing I wanted to pick up in Japan was a Nikon camera, one like the UPI reporter was carrying around back at LZ Leslie. Strange how those news guys would do anything to get a photo, even at the risk of getting their balls blown off. *Maybe someday*, I thought, *when I get out of this shit, I'll become a photographer.*

After breakfast, I said my goodbyes to Curly and the kid from Georgia and went back to my room to take another swig of saki. Would I make good on my promises to pick up shit for my guys back in the Nam? I had an entire laundry list of shit to pick up. I'd take a cab to downtown Yokohama and look around, I thought, maybe find that camera. I'd have plenty of time since I wouldn't hook up with Michiko until around four.

I found a camera shop next to the port, ships and tugboats lining the docks to the northwest as far as I could see. The shop was in a mall cozied up next to the edge of the water. In the display case, a price tag of 60,000 yen for a Nikon F seemed reasonable for something I'd dreamed of for so long. "How much for the 105mm lenses?" I asked the middle-aged man behind the counter. Agreeing to the price on both items, I handed over my money as he slipped my purchases into a bag.

I'd fantasized about a Nikon ever since I saw that movie *Blow-Up* with David Hemmings and Vanessa Redgrave. What was it about a camera and lens? What possessed the news guys back in the Nam to risk their lives for an image, the female photographer to run around with combat units to get that one shot, maybe a magazine cover? How did she get that shot of those gooks on the other side of the rice paddy shooting at us? What motivated her? Was it fame? Was it the dollars? Was it to show the world what war looks like? Was it merely to document the carnage? I think not.

It felt good to have something of quality tucked under my arm. I left the camera shop in search of a bar. Time was slipping by fast; I needed a drink. I walked along the meandering streets past a pizza joint, a Chinese restaurant, and other establishments with signs I couldn't read. Two or three blocks from the edge of the salt water and ocean air, I could hear music coming from a plaster-covered building with a structure next door that looked like a lighthouse with a tower on top. As I entered the establishment, I saw there was a bar off to the left, tables and chairs on the right, and four guys playing jazz over in the corner. One was playing the piano, one playing the stand-up bass, another a Spanish-style guitar, and one on the drums. It seemed a bit early for a band, with only a handful of patrons, but it sounded OK—I wasn't a fan of jazz unless it was Miles Davis, Dizzy Gillespie, or Wes Montgomery.

I sat at the bar alone and drank beer until midafternoon. It was like I couldn't get enough. The room started spinning. It wouldn't stop. I walked around the block—it was cold—hoping it would sober me up. Sitting back down at the bar, I ordered another beer. I drank half of it and grabbed a cab back to the hotel. It was still relatively early, but I was done.

I met my lady friend, grabbed some chow, and crashed.

The sun's rays filtered through the blinds, interrupting my sleep; morning and a hangover stared back at me from the mirror as I took a leak. It pissed me off I'd wasted the night before being drunk. I poured a glass of saki from the nearly three-foot-high bottle—the Breakfast of Champions.

In the lobby, a salesman dealing in suits and overcoats approached me—a twenty-something fellow whose English was a cut above the normal. Since I'd bought a green suit in Taipei, I might as well buy one here—after all, they were tailor-made. Only this time, I added a cashmere overcoat. What the hell, it was only blood money. I liked this guy Hiroto; he was inquisitive, funny, and informative.

"Have you looked around Tokyo yet?" Hiroto asked.

"No, just when I flew in," I said.

"How about a tour? I can show you the sights."

"Yeah, sure. When?"

"How about tonight?"

Nighttime came soon enough, and the two of us took off for the big city . . . not that Yokohama isn't. I wasn't really sure why he offered, but I couldn't pass up the chance to see the sights. Downtown Tokyo was busy, neon lights everywhere. It reminded me of 42nd Street in New York, or maybe Las Vegas. It certainly beat the crap out of the black nights in a foxhole with green tracer rounds whizzing overhead.

Around nine o'clock, we stopped by his office and walked up a flight of stairs to the second floor. We entered a large room with desks scattered about, with his fellow salesmen milling around: he introduced me to his comrades as they were taking a break, eating sushi.

"What are they eating?" I asked.

"Sushi, do you want to try some?" Hiroto asked.

"No, thanks," I said. What the hell? It looked raw. First, there was the dried squid in the vending machine back at the hotel, and now raw fish. That was some strange shit these people ate.

"When was the last time you've talked to your parents?" he asked.

It surprised me. *That's an odd question*, I thought. Trying to recall the exact date, I answered: "The last time I talked to either one of my parents was in February of last year. I said goodbye to my dad at LAX when he dropped me off," I said. The image of him walking away filled my thoughts—his driving the seventy miles back home alone in his '57 VW saddened me.

"Would you like to call them from here and let them know you're OK?" he asked.

Looking at him and not answering right away, I finally asked, "What time would it be there?"

"Early morning, it's nearly ten o'clock here. It'd be close to six in the morning."

Hiroto told me not to worry about the cost, that he'd just mark it down as a business expense.

He called the international operator, and within a few minutes, I awoke my dad. It took him a few minutes to get to the phone.

"Hi, Dad, this is Jim, I'm calling from Japan."

It was a brief conversation. "Are you OK?" Small talk. I worried about the expense and my indebtedness to Hiroto.

"Keep your chin up, Jimmy; it won't be long now," Dad said.

"No, it won't."

The conversation was short and unsubstantial, then we hung up.

Twenty minutes later, we were back motoring around Yokohama. Around two in the morning, he pulled into a parking spot in front of a coffee shop. "Geez, this place never slows down, does it?" I asked as we got out of the Toyota.

"No, people work all the time."

We took a seat at the counter, ordering coffee and talking about the US and where I grew up. What was it like to live there? Then he leaned over and asked, "What do you think about Hiroshima and Nagasaki? What do you think about that?" he asked. The question stunned me. Like it came out of the blue. What the hell kind of question was that? I hadn't really thought about it. As I looked around the cafe, I saw I was the only round-eye in the joint. Images of mushroom clouds and fried bodies filled my mind.

"I don't know. I really hadn't thought about it. It was horrible, that's all I know," I said lamely.

Hiroto didn't push the point and let the question die. He turned back to his cup of coffee and stared straight ahead. A pregnant moment in time, I'd say. I was hoping no one in the coffee shop spoke English.

We called it a night and left for the hotel. After all, it was the middle of the night.

A couple of days later, Hiroto dropped off the gray suit and black cashmere overcoat. I was feeling guilty and grateful for his generosity in letting me call my folks, showing me around Tokyo and Yokohama. I pulled out my wallet and took out thirty dollars and handed it to him.

"It's for the telephone call," I said.

He looked at me for a moment and hesitated to take the money. After my insistence, he finally took it. As he left, it occurred to me I had insulted him. I wasn't able to accept his gift.

JAPAN

With light rays streaming through the window, illuminating the bottle of saki in the room's corner, it was time to start the day. What crazy-ass thing could possibly happen today? Hiroshima and Nagasaki, what the fuck. A glass of rice wine sounded good. A bath in the funny square tub, catching up with the guys, shooting the breeze, and deciding on something to do.

With the morning flying by, it was time for that little bar down by the waterfront. I couldn't get any of the other shitheads to go along. Fuck 'em; I didn't like 'em anyhow.

The waterfront bar felt faintly calming, familiar—a handful of patrons and a beautiful young woman sitting at a round wooden table. I took a seat at the bar and ordered a beer. Taking a sip, I glanced over at the sweet young honey. Definitely a cut above Michiko, but not by much; she made the first move and asked if I would like to join her.

"Sure," I said as I pulled out a chair and sat down.

"What'll you have?" I said. She turned and called to the bartender, ordering a drink. I couldn't tell what it was, but I knew I was on the hook paying for it.

An hour passed, and my money was getting a little tight.

"Have you ever been to the USO club?" she asked.

"I didn't know they had one."

"It's not far from here, but I can't go with you unless you pay."

"How much?"

"Sixteen hundred yen."

I figured what the hell and gave her the money. She excused herself and disappeared into an office at the back of the bar. Shit, she'd grabbed my money, and now what? But a couple of minutes later, there she was.

"Let's go," she said.

A few miles away, the USO club was jamming and loud, servicemen of all stripes sitting with their buddies or hookers. "The band sounds good, yes?" she asked.

"Oh, they're OK," I said, thinking they pretty much sucked, but so what. Bored and wondering what my next move was, I took another swig of beer. Then the sweet young thing reached under the table and grabbed my thigh.

"You want me?" she asked as she squeezed my thigh.

"Yeah, sure."

"Fifteen dollars. I show you good time."

What the fuck, I'd just paid her fifteen bucks.

"I already paid for you."

"No. No, you paid the bar so I could come with you."

Mad as hell, I got up and started for the door. Fuck this.

She followed me out as I flagged a cab. I didn't tell her, but I didn't have fifteen dollars. I had thirteen dollars.

"How much you pay."

"Ten dollars."

She told me her name, but I didn't pay attention. All I knew was she was willing to take the ten-spot.

We got into the back seat, and she told the driver where to go. Uphill, downhill, houses and small businesses on both sides of the street. I had no idea where I was or where we were going. I was just getting a little concerned when we stopped in front of an establishment, a Japanese-style motel, traditional, I'd say. The beds were on the floor, the pillows filled with rice; there was a large community bath. Very exotic.

She was worth every nickel I paid her. I rolled over and passed out for the night. The next morning, there was no girl, no message, no nothing. I put on my clothes and left. Opening the door to bright sunlight, I saw nothing resembling a landmark in sight. Where the fuck was I? People walking by wore masks over their mouths. The pollution wasn't like in LA; perhaps they were afraid of inhaling germs. Who knew, and who cared. It was strange—alien. Then I noticed a busy street five or six blocks to the south—or what seemed south.

I waved down a taxi on the busy street, and he pulled over and reached across to roll down the window. He asked me where I was going in Japanese; at least, that's what I thought he was asking. *Fuck, where am I going? What the hell?* I couldn't remember the name of the hotel. Fishing around in my pocket, I found a business card with the hotel's address on it and handed it to him.

He smiled and motioned for me to get in. On the way to the hotel, I hoped I had enough money to cover the cost of the cab. How much was it going to cost me? What happens when you can't pay the tab?

Luckily, I had just enough to cover the expense. Feeling fortunate to make it back, I rode the elevator up to my floor. The elevator door opened, and I started for my room. Michiko and her lady friends were in the hall. They all started yelling at me.

"You butterfly, GI, you butterfly, you bad." They kept repeating it like a chant as I made my way to my room.

"No, I didn't butterfly," I protested.

"No, no, you butterfly," they insisted.

They had me dead to rights. And they knew it.

37

Cam Ranh Bay

I was in Cam Ranh Bay again, a beautiful oasis perched on the edge of the South China Sea. Perhaps I could hide out here for a few days before returning to An Khê. With less than a month left in-country, who in their right mind would return early enough to be sent back to the field?

Dan, a pudgy kid from Alabama, had sat next to me on the plane back from Japan. He was in an artillery outfit. It made sense, given his bulk. After checking in, we bought a bottle of Chivas Regal from the PX to facilitate an evening of reflection and worry about the days ahead. Assigned to the top floor of a two-story barracks, we sat out on the step at the top of the landing and told stories, sharing sips of Scotch.

An hour passed, the sun sliding down below the horizon, the bottle half-empty, the light from the barracks shining overhead, the temperature just right. Our conversation ranged between war and an uncertain future. Dan had six months to go and I had just days. The safety of the moment would soon disappear like the sun, in a day or two. Come morning, it was back to the shit. Dan on his flight to hell and me on mine. We finished off the bottle of Scotch and crashed.

The next morning, I reported for departure back to An Khê but was so hungover, I figured I'd stay another day. So what if I was AWOL, fuck 'em. Surveying the area, I didn't see Dan. So, I assumed he made his flight.

The following day, after another night at the club, I made the flight back to An Khê and my unit.

"Get up, get up, up and at 'em," yelled the base camp staff sergeant—the SOB in charge of company operation in base camp.

"Fuck you, asshole!" yelled someone in the middle of the barracks.

"Who said that? Who said that?" the staff sergeant insisted.

Silence.

A few minutes later, all of us lined up in formation, the staff sergeant started calling names of those ordered back to their units in the field. When and where to report, shit like that.

"When you hear your name, sound off," yelled the staff sergeant.

Sure enough, he yelled out my name.

I yelled out, "Yo." So, there it was. But, it being mere days before I'd be sent back here, I decided to save the army the expense and spent the next few days at the Red Cross center. Skip morning formation; I would grab a little chow and sneak off to the center, then come back in the evenings for a night of drinking. The only fly in the ointment was when I rounded a corner and ran into the first sergeant. He looked up and acknowledged me and kept moving. I'm guessing he never expected me to return to the field. I'd heard he promoted one of the new guys to take over my job as acting communications chief. I'd had the job for four months but wasn't promoted to sergeant. Of course, I was never hesitant to voice my displeasure with the army.

While I was hanging out in An Khê waiting for the final order, the order to go home, a bunch of scared-to-death newbies showed up in the barracks one night. All of them worried about their future. They were all ears when Casey assured them they would do just fine. I didn't know why Casey was in base camp, but there he was, holding court.

"Don't sweat it, guys. It'll be all right. You'll see," said Casey, reassuring them.

What he didn't tell them was that every time we'd move to a new location, when we'd set up a new camp in the field, he would become disoriented. In and amongst the intermittent grenades we threw during the night, you might hear Casey wake up screaming. It had nothing to do with his recent episode with gonorrhea, grenades, or ghosts. The glue he'd sniffed as a teenager back in New York City would cause him to do this. It never lasted very long, but on this occasion, it was his first night back at base camp, a new location. I felt certain Casey's reassuring words fell short of the mark when the midnight hour arrived.

A week later, I had my orders in hand and my pecker inspected, dressed in a khaki uniform. It was goodbye to An Khê and hello to Cam Ranh Bay. The big bird taking us home was on its way. The last day, hour, and minute had arrived. As I lifted my foot off the ground to climb the stairs, I noticed Eight-ball climbing the stairs ahead of me. I hadn't noticed him until then.

As we took off, I snapped my last photo of the bloodstained land. The realization of having made it out sunk in. A window seat on the left side of the plane, as we headed north, allowed me to look out over the horizon. Somewhere out there, my comrades in arms would be digging foxholes, blowing up air mattresses, and wishing they were in my shoes. Hopefully, they would be someday soon.

After a brief stop for fuel in Japan, then flying over the Aleutian Islands, we landed at McChord Air Force Base in Washington State. It was February 10 when we took off and February 10 when we landed. The international dateline made for a very long day and night. The army picked us up and transported us to Fort Lewis. For some, it was the end of active duty; others received orders to a new duty station.

It was time to complete paperwork—an all-day affair. Among the day's agenda: a steak dinner, a medical exam, an opportunity to re-up for another tour of duty. Everyone turned it down, even Eight-ball the lifer that day, February 10. He'd had enough.

Everything was going along smoothly until the medic, taking my blood pressure, looked at me and said, "Your blood pressure is too high." He seemed to be confused as to what to do. Then he got the bright idea of having me lie down. I was happy to oblige. No way did I want to be held over. Fuck that. Fortunately, the medic could record a decent number, and I was off to the next task.

My final hour of active duty had arrived, and I boarded the bus to SeaTac in my newly issued class A uniform. Eight-ball went his way, and I went mine. I boarded the flight headed for San Francisco International.

III

Part Three

38

Uncle Nick

After a night in San Francisco, I flew home. But home was awkward, and I felt out of place. So, when I heard about my cousin getting married in a couple of weeks up in the Seattle area, I was happy to escape and fly back to the northwest.

After the wedding, I hitched a ride with my aunt and uncle back to Southern California, in the back seat of their Plymouth sedan. Uncle Nick, with his dark, almost black hair, was resting his right hand on the Brodie knob (some call it a spinner or suicide knob) on the steering wheel. In his other hand was an unfiltered Camel cigarette. He was a chain smoker. My aunt was quiet in the passenger seat. I never understood why my uncle liked Plymouths. Chevy, Ford, those were my preference, my favorites. Although Plymouths had nifty push buttons on the left-hand side of the dash for changing gears—innovation, maybe that's what Uncle Nick liked. Centered on the dash was the ever-present compass. Every car he owned—that I can remember—had a compass. I figured it had to do with his time in the Army Air Corps, being a pilot and all. The only annoying behavior to me was his constant adjustment of speed. It was like the gas pedal needed movement; otherwise, it might stick.

We were south of Portland now, with Mt. Hood off to the East, standing alone in the afternoon sky. Wonderful.

I thought about our family gatherings in Monrovia and the big table. Before my war, the last time I broke bread with aunts, uncles, and cousins, we were all seated at the same table. The little folding table had been stowed in the closet. All of us had graduated to the adult table and conversation. When Uncle Nick finished his last bite, he'd set down his fork, grabbed his pack of Camels, and, with a quick shake, picked the tallest one and lit up whether anyone else had finished eating. It seemed selfish. Mixing mashed potatoes and cigarette smoke irritated me.

Nevertheless, I liked sitting next to him. He had a wicked intellect and a quick mind. No matter the subject of conversation, his biting, sarcastic commentary—audible only to those closest to him—made for an entertaining afternoon.

Before moving to Monrovia, years ago, Uncle Nick had moved to a new house in Duarte. I—a snot-nosed kid—was visiting for the weekend. Uncle Nick had just planted a new lawn, the little blades two inches high and sparse. I was riding my cousin's tricycle and lost control and wheeled into the yard. Uncle Nick shot out of the house and yelled something. I don't remember the words, but his eyes, burning eyes, stared into my soul, scaring the crap out of me.

Like all them old-timers from WWII, he was a hard man to get to know; he didn't talk about the war, he didn't talk about being in the Army Air Corps or flying the Burma Hump. I still know little about his life. A pharmacist by trade, he busted his ass to get through USC's pharmacy school. He didn't lack for smarts.

We rolled into Denny's in Redding, California; it was time to stretch our legs and grab a bite. The waitress seated us next to the window overlooking the parking lot. It was a sunny afternoon, and I searched the menu for something to satisfy my hunger. A glass of ice water sat in front of me—a luxury a short while ago. It felt good to be home with my aunt and uncle. The words spoken were pleasant, non confrontational, and superficial. It didn't matter. The body language, the occasional glance, the unwritten communication soothed me somehow.

"I'll have a hamburger, fries, and a Coke."

"And you?" the waitress asked my uncle.

And so it went until the plates lay empty except for a bit of ketchup, a burnt fry, and Uncle Nick smoking a Camel. As we left, I noticed he didn't leave a tip. I'd forgotten that about him. He didn't believe in tipping. He figured they got a paycheck. After all, his customers didn't leave him a tip for filling their prescriptions.

On the road again, sitting in the back seat, I watched the planted fields of the Central Valley pass by.

MacArthur. I thought back to the story Uncle Nick had told me about him. About the time he was flying him somewhere. Maybe over the South China Sea, perhaps over the Burma Hump. I was speculating; I couldn't remember. Then I remembered his comment about him being a real son of a bitch. His words spoke volumes to me now, the arrogance of some commanders.

The image of General Westmoreland's arrival at LZ Ross came to mind, Westy popping out of his chopper and climbing into the back seat of a jeep, riding around, surveying his minions. Forty-five minutes later, he climbed back into his chopper and disappeared. The brass and the press only showed up when the fireworks were about to begin. Like MacArthur leaving his troops in the Philippines, Westmoreland did the same.

Then, a few days later, I had sat in the orderly room with Bennington, where I was preparing to go on leave. Both of us were listening to the dispatches from Ross: the Chinook being shot down, the rescue attempts to find the survivors, and my guys surrounded, trying to make it back to base as best they could. I never learned who made it back and who didn't. Soon, I'd be in Japan sipping Manhattans, clueless, a list tucked into my shirt pocket of items they wanted me to pick up. Items like a deck of cards of naked ladies, a *Playboy* magazine, and other things I never picked up.

When I returned, Bennington told me about our company being moved to fight outside the walls of the old Imperial City of Hue, trying to block the NVA from entering the battle where the Marines were fighting inside the walls.

As I focused on the fields and crops racing by—empty fields, no one lying face down, bleeding—I thought of the battalion commander sending Greeley, Mason, and Ryan to be pinned down in a rice paddy without their gear, hugging the ground, hoping a bullet didn't find its mark. Short of ammo, surrounded, sneaking through enemy lines under cover of darkness on a moonless night, leaving the dead behind. It had to be the longest twenty-four hours of the war for my poor bastards, my brothers-in-arms.

Had I picked up the items they requested, it might have transported their minds away from the ever-present executioner, providing an escape if only for a moment, even a split second. Only, I couldn't find the time. I was too busy drinking and playing with my lady friends. My mission of fulfilling their modest requests went unanswered. I had no excuse, nothing I could say, and no apologies would squelch the disappointment in myself.

How many survived? Who survived? The twist of fate, the arbitrary circumstances of who lives and who dies. Which of my friends were resting their heads on a small pillow in a box covered with red, white, and blue? I had no answers, just winter crops planted in long rows, the hum of the engine droning on, the compass registering south. Our destination was only a few hours away.

39

Helen

At the Inland Center Mall Dunkin' Donuts, draining the last few drops from a cup of coffee, I used the receipt from the bookstore I'd visited as a marker in Robert Heinlein's book *Stranger in a Strange Land.* I got up and pushed the chair under the table and made my way toward the exit. Strolling down the promenade toward me was none other than my high school sweetheart, Helen. I'd heard somewhere she had divorced William and was staying with her folks. She smiled and greeted me with, "Hi, how are you? It's been so long."

"Yes, yes, it has. Fine. I'm doing fine."

We stood there awkwardly standing there, fumbling for words, and she invited me to visit her at her parents' place.

"My parents would love to see you."

"Sure, that would be great," I said with a smile. "I'd love to see your folks, too." I remembered the image of her dad sitting there in the living room, a medical book in his hands, the light shining down from the lamp standing next to him. Years ago, I had been a patient of his. He had an office just south of Foothill Boulevard on Riverside Avenue. I'd awakened one morning, unable to hear out of one ear, and he was kind enough to work me in that morning and clean the wax out of my ear.

They lived in a big Spanish-style house with a tennis court in the backyard. Not everything was peaches and roses in their family, though Helen's younger sister had died of a childhood cancer a couple of years earlier.

"So, are you staying with them now?" I asked.

"Yes, for the time being. I'm going back to San Francisco State in the fall to finish up."

"Wonderful!" I said then paused for a moment. "I think I still have your parents' phone number somewhere. They're in the book, right?"

"Yes, of course," she replied. Then she added, "Don't wait too long, OK?"

"I won't," I said, then she continued on her way.

After a few feet, I took a quick look back, hoping she wouldn't catch me. She still walked like an angel, gliding across the finished concrete floor with ease. She had such a graceful way about her.

Reaching the exit, I had no intention of calling. My light-colored Volkswagen Bug sat in the afternoon sun, the temperature already above 90 degrees. Sliding the key into the handle, twisting it, unlocking the door, I looked across the roof at the mountain range to the north and I thought of the bombs dropping, pounding, penetrating, now silent.

40

Mrs. Smith

On a Saturday afternoon, sitting in a small bar located a few miles from home, I took another swig of beer and began filling out the paperwork for the upcoming college semester. The smoke from my Viceroy cigarette was burning above a half dozen butts lying in the ashtray. I figured it was time to move on and continue my studies. Only, my mind had trouble concentrating on the paperwork and I found myself trying to decide which titty bar was best: Sinners or The Booby Trap. As a part-time salesman at Standard Brands Paint Store on E Street, I spent most evenings alone hanging out at those bars on Waterman Avenue.

Since neither of my parents smoked or drank, I'm sure the folks weren't pleased when I came home late reeking of both booze and cigarettes. Although neither would say a word, it made me feel uncomfortable, and it was time to unburden them.

I found an ad in the *San Bernardino Sun-Telegram* of rentals next to the college.

A complex with six units, three buildings shaped in a horseshoe facing South Eureka Avenue, looked promising. I found the office door and knocked. Mrs. Smith, a widow, answered the door.

"Do you have an apartment to rent?" I asked.

"Why, yes," she replied. "Right across from me."

She pointed to the apartment catty-corner from her. I immediately liked her. She was small-framed, short, wiry, with graying hair and a pleasant personality; I felt she wouldn't make a nuisance of herself.

Except for the landlady, college students occupied the other units, all younger than me.

We agreed on the rent, and I wrote her a check—done deal.

I moved in and settled in, and classes started.

Mrs. Smith was so nonintrusive, I hardly knew she lived thirty feet away. No visitors, either, not even her son. I thought she mentioned he worked for the San Bernardino Police Department as a detective. Strange, I thought. I didn't pry, and I didn't ask about her past.

When I walked back from class at San Bernardino Valley College— just across the street—on day one, she was out pulling a few weeds and greeted me and asked how I was making out.

"Oh, fine. Thanks for asking. How are you doing?" I countered.

"As well as can be expected, for an old lady."

As the days went by, she inquired about my past. A bit nosy, I thought. I told her of my time in Vietnam and growing up in the bedroom community of Rialto.

The idea floated in my mind that maybe she would like to see some photos from the Nam.

"Would you like to see some of my slides from the war?" I asked.

"Why, yes," she replied.

With nothing planned for the evening, I said, "Come over about seven—after it gets dark, so the slides will show up—and I'll set up the projector."

She seemed excited about the invitation.

"See you then."

Darkness came, and Mrs. Smith knocked on my door, came in, and sat down on the small couch, one of those Swedish-style pieces: skinny legs, elegant and simple, but cheap. The white wall would serve as a screen. The projector had a little plastic handle; you pushed in to center the slide in front of the bulb, then pulled out to catch the next slide. A cheap slide projector for sure, but it was the only way for people to see the tiny 110mm slides. The slides came from the camera that had gone missing back in the graveyard. The slides were way too small to see much with the naked eye.

Mrs. Smith wore a floral-print dress with large buttons down the front, something she probably picked up at the Sears, Roebuck store down on 2nd Street. I offered her a soda, which she accepted.

As the images appeared on the wall, I told her the story behind each one.

"That's Casey from New York City, a funny kid. You would have liked him. We're filling sandbags for a bunker. Sergeant Morgan, the one laughing, is from Mississippi, a worthless human being."

The sound of another slide moving into the projector accompanied another story, a bit of what was going on.

"That's Lieutenant Everly, the blond next to the mortar tube with his fingers in his ears. He's no longer with us. He and the others were ambushed and killed not long after this photo was taken."

She said nothing, absorbing the commentary. It went like that for a few more slides.

"That's the view from LZ Leslie."

"Beautiful," she whispered.

"Yes, in the evening, everyone settled down; the views were breathtaking. You'd wonder how such a beautiful place could exist—the colors, the evening skies reflecting off the mosaic of rice paddies, the tall mountains serving as a backdrop. Beautiful," I said, echoing her words.

The next slide was a jungle scene with more shades of green than you can imagine. Then, it occurred to me: I wondered how many people she saw reflecting off the white wall?

She studied a bit, then said, "Two."

"No, there are five." I got up from my chair and pointed out where they were. I'd lived with dangers hidden in a sea of green, and I knew she couldn't find them all.

The slides spent, her soda consumed, the conversation at a standstill, she thanked me for showing her my photos.

A couple of days went by, and I hadn't seen her. I thought it odd. Around 10 a.m. Saturday morning, I heard some strangers across the way. I didn't recognize the men—two of them, dressed in dark slacks and white shirts. Then I noticed one of them had a badge on his belt. Janet, one of the college students, joined them. I could see them talking. They appeared concerned and puzzled, fumbling for guidance.

I opened my door and asked Janet what was going on.

"It's Mrs. Smith; she's dead. She hung herself in the doorway of her bedroom." As she pointed to one of the two strangers, she said, "That one is her son."

I reentered my apartment, walked to the fridge, pulled out an Oly. Searching for the church key among all the dirty dishes in my sink, I found it lying in plain sight. Walking back to the living room, sitting down on the only chair, I forced the tip of the church key into the lid of the cold beer. It was not even noon; it was time to get started. Turning the beer around, I punctured the other side of the lid. It allowed the liquid to go down faster. As I was thinking, questioning why she would have done such a thing, a thought entered my mind: "Fuck, death followed me home."

That night at Sinners, I ordered a pitcher of beer from where I was seated next to the stage. With music playing on the jukebox and a nude dancer doing her thing, I hadn't paid attention to the other patrons in the bar until the waitress startled me when she sidled up next to me and licked my ear and whispered, "I'm collecting money for the jukebox." Then—as I looked around—I realized the place was full of Hells Angels. I was so loaded when I came in, I hadn't noticed them or the motorcycles parked outside. I handed a buck to the licker, finished my beer, and headed home.

41

The Letter

"How are you? How is school?" my mother asked as she stood in front of the stove, an apron tied around her neck and waist.

"Fine. Everything is fine," I replied. Of course, nothing was fine.

It was Sunday afternoon, and I felt an obligation to visit the folks, pick up whatever mail might still be coming to their address. A roast was resting in a pot on the stovetop, the yellow Formica breakfast table set with colorful Fiestaware—mostly orange and green. It was Sunday dinner. I sat down on a chair with chrome legs and a plastic-covered cushion. Looking out of the south window at the lemon bush in bloom with small white flowers, I thought about the lemon pies Mom made from that lemon bush. Wonderful pies. The recollection of C rations and powdered eggs turned green from the aluminum mermite cans gave way to a bit of comfort as I studied the bees pollinating the flowers. Images of my childhood drifted through my mind. Although I still heard odd noises here and there, setting off twinges of fear I couldn't control, I appreciated the familiar surroundings.

The fumes of a diesel truck, the sudden flash of sunlight by a passing car window, and a keen awareness of my environment told me I wasn't right. I wasn't like the other kids I'd grown up with. Now I was old enough to buy a beer, old enough to vote, and old enough to carry the scars of combat. Always sitting with my back against the wall, eyeballing the nearest exit, I was alone and distant in my mind. I spent a lot of time self-medicating.

I know the folks were disappointed that I'd not seen fit to attend church service. They had summoned the church members to welcome me home and back into the fold, but it felt awkward. I couldn't relate. I couldn't help that. Reengaging that part of my past wasn't happening. There was life before the Nam and then life after, and the church didn't figure into it.

"I've got a letter here for you. It's on the dining room table. The potatoes will be ready soon."

I'd been home for six months—compared to the Nam, time was sliding by in slow motion.

Mother picked up the letter from the table in the dining room and handed it to me. As I took it, I noticed it was postmarked Kansas, a six-cent blue stamp with a moon aligned in the upper left corner and the word liberty, in white letters, centered at the bottom. My name and address were written in cursive. I figured it for a woman's handwriting. Who the fuck did I know in Kansas? I unfolded it; it read in part:

You don't know me, but I'm hoping you knew my son. My husband and I live on a farm in western Kansas, where we raised our son: Jerome Richardson. If you haven't heard, he was recently killed in Vietnam. While going through his belongings, I found your name and address written on a slip of paper. I was hoping you might be able to tell us something about what happened. Did you serve with him in Vietnam? Were you with him when he died? If you served with him, can you tell us anything, anything at all? We're heartbroken and grief-stricken, and any information you can provide would mean everything to us. I understand you might still be in Vietnam, but I'm hoping, at some point in the future, you will see this letter and respond.

I hope this letter finds you in good health.

Sincerely,
 Martha Richardson

I folded the letter up and slipped it back into its envelope and laid it back on the table. Mother was poking the scalloped potatoes with a fork. Then she proclaimed, "Dinner's ready."

After dinner, I grabbed the letter and some leftovers and headed out the door to my VW. Climbing into the driver's seat, I laid the letter down on the passenger seat. Turning the engine over, I thought about the letter and what she wrote, then I depressed the clutch and shifted into first gear. It was back to Berdoo and a stop at the liquor store to purchase a couple of six-packs.

How the hell would I answer that letter? What the fuck could I say?

Opening the door to my apartment, I found the Corona portable typewriter sitting next to the wall. Taking the cover off and positioning it on the coffee table, I ratcheted a sheet of typing paper and started typing.

Dear Mr. and Mrs. Richardson,

Please let me start with: I am so sorry for your loss.
 Yes, I did know your son. We met at the bar adjoining the dining room of the Hilton Inn at the San Francisco Airport. He was leaving the next day for Alameda naval station, and I was on the final leg of my journey home

after returning from Vietnam.

He was obviously very inquisitive about his future, what he might expect, what it was like, and so on. I liked him immediately. As I recall, he said he was from western Kansas. A few years ago, at a party in La Jolla, a kid was visiting from Kansas. One of the guys at the party was a professor friend from one of the nearby colleges and peppered the kid with endless questions about farming wheat, how many bushels per acre, ballpark figure per bushel, and so on. So when I found out your son was a wheat farmer, the memory of that party came to mind. The longer I talked with your son, the more I knew he was a straight shooter, a man of his word, and a friend to trust—a highly prized attribute in combat. I was hoping for the best.

I don't know much about wheat farming, but I know this spring when the first leaf of wheat pushes through the cold dirt looking for life, your son had a hand in all that, that first sheath, that first sprig, and the promise of a plentiful harvest. Hopefully, with the help of spring rains and the late summer sun, a wave of amber will lighten your burden and you'll see the wind brush across his face.

Sincerely,

I couldn't think of any more to write. I wondered if I'd even mail it. I sat in the field many a day and spilled my guts with ink on paper, then tucked it away, never to be mailed. I knew people wanted to know more, but I was powerless to tell them. I didn't have the tools.

I knew as loved ones laid their heads down at day's end, worrying about their flesh and blood half a world away, quieting their minds so they could drift off to sleep was never easy. They, too, were cursed. The fog of not knowing, the agonizing quest for answers, the midnight hour never-ending. Like me, they wanted more, needed more, more than Walter Cronkite and the evening news.

Punching a hole in another beer, I sat on my couch, watching the six o'clock news on the thirteen-inch black-and-white screen of my portable TV, images in shades of gray. Wounded soldiers carried across battlefields, sounds of gunfire coming from the tiny speaker with a man in a suit planted behind a desk speaking words without knowledge. Meaningless commentary, photos, and videos, that's all we were, nothing more, just words printed in black and white, devoid of any true understanding. I wanted to tell the stories. I needed to tell the stories, but in the end, did anyone really want to hear them? I think not. There was no glory— no victory parades, no welcome home signs displayed on Main Street, the shiny medals tucked away; I felt doomed to a quagmire of painful thoughts locked in a brain teetering on the edge of a bone-handle straight razor. I was a stranger pretending to be home.

Printed in Dunstable, United Kingdom